THE DRUNK DIET

THE DRUNK DIET

How I Lost 40 Pounds . . . Wasted

A MEMOIR

Lüc Carl

ST. MARTIN'S PRESS
NEW YORK

No alcohol beverage manufacturer has endorsed or sponsored this book.

Photos on pages ii, 147 (both), 149 (all), 154, 166 (both), 157 (both), 158 courtesy of Terry Richardson. Photos on pages 4, 7, 12–13, 17, 19, 20, 22, 30, 37, 39, 62, 129, 142, 167, 171, and 241 courtesy of the author. Photo on page 178 courtesy of brightroom.com. Photo on page 220 courtesy of www.Marathon-Photos.com.

www.stmartins.com

ISBN: 978-1-250-00182-5 (hardcover)
ISBN: 978-1-250-00182-5 (e-book)

First Edition: March 2012

10 9 8 7 6 5 4 3 2 1

To anyone who's ever
wanted something better …

CONTENTS

PART II
Iron Maiden Changed My Life
Or, How Not to Look Like an Asshole
When You're Working Out

MEDICAL DISCLAIMER

Dear Asshole,

So, my publisher told me I have to include a medical disclaimer for all you morons out there. You know, "This book is not intended to replace the advice of your own physician or health-care professional; you should consult a doctor, or some other qualified dumbass, before making any changes to your diet or workout routine," blah, blah, blah. Listen:

I used to get drunk at work, close up the bar, put on "Eye of the Tiger," and do one-arm push-ups to impress whatever ladies were still hanging around after the gate went down. Then one Saturday morning I woke up, and I couldn't move my right shoulder. In fact, my shoulder was totally fucked for nearly two weeks—all because I was a drunk asshole trying to show off in a bar at four in the morning.

The Drunk Diet is not a diet plan that involves getting drunk and then going to the gym to do some cross-training, ok? The point is *not* to get drunk, and then get in shape. And anyone who thinks I'm advocating alcoholism is an idiot. Everybody knows that you can't knock back six shots of Jack and then go for a three-mile run. *The Drunk Diet* is me being a smart-ass and giving the finger to every other "[fill in the blank] Diet" book on the shelf.

This is my story. If you don't like it, write your own fucking book.

The Downward Spiral

I t was the day before my twenty-eighth birthday. I was in the Bahamas with two of my closest friends, Newman and Tony. After spending the entire afternoon drinking cold beers on the beach, we took a cab to a nice hotel, which was about fifteen miles away from our shitty hotel, and fucked around in its casino—eating steaks, drinking, smoking cigars, and raising hell for a couple of hours. It was a Monday night, and we needed to make it back to our shitty hotel in time to put bets down on the *Monday Night Football* game. (We knew that if we stayed to watch the game at the nice hotel, we'd be way too fucked up to ever make it home.) So, we cashed in our chips, got in a cab, and headed back to the broke side of the island where we belonged.

We had already been drinking all day, as we did nearly every day, but we needed a little something to get us over the top. So Tony started chatting up the cab driver, asking where we could score some weed. "No problem," said the cabbie. "I'll take you to a guy." Since the game was starting in fifteen minutes, we told the driver to drop Newman and me off at the hotel so we could get our bets in before kickoff. Tony gave me a hundred bucks, told me to bet fifty dollars on whichever team I liked—I, of course, bet the whole hundred—and stayed in the cab. Newman and I, meanwhile, placed our own hundred-dollar bets, ordered some more cocktails, and sat down to watch the game.

By the end of the first quarter, still no Tony. We were in a foreign country, with no cell phones and enough long hair and tattoos to attract more attention than the Bearded Woman in Coney Island. But Tony is a tough dude, I thought. He can handle a couple of drug dealers—there's one on every street corner back home in Brooklyn. Also, we'd been drinking since noon, so we were past the point of really giving a shit about *anything*, except playing cards and ordering more beers. (In fact, I later realized that I'd been so wasted when I talked to my football guy from back home that I placed the bets on the *wrong* team; we ended up losing the three hundred dollars.)

At the start of the second quarter, we sat down to play blackjack. Finally, Tony showed up.

"What the fuck took you so long?" I asked.

Tony threw his hands in the air. "I got an AK-47 pulled on my ass!"

Apparently, when the cab pulled up to the dealer's house, two huge guys came out to investigate. Bohemian locals, Tony said. Both dressed in military-like gear, stood shoulder to shoulder with their arms crossed against their chests. Once they got closer, they each stepped aside to reveal a third man, armed with a fully automatic machine gun aimed directly at Tony's face.

"Oh, my God," I said. "What the fuck did you do? I would have shit my pants!"

"I *did* shit my pants!" he screamed. Luckily, the dealers had only wanted to scare the white boy who had enough balls to come into their neighborhood to score drugs. They let him go without beating the shit out of him first.

"So . . . you're telling me you didn't get the weed?" I asked, when he finished telling me the story.

"Of course, I got it!" he said. "Let's go up to the room and roll a joint."

We didn't have any rolling papers, so we ripped out the first page of the Book of Luke from the hotel Bible. Then we stole some portable speakers from the room and headed out to the beach. We had an iPod full of Rock 'N' Roll, a bottle of whiskey, and our bag of weed, and we were looking for trouble. It was just another day in my crazy, booze-soaked life. The only surprising thing is that I can actually remember it.

You see, by late 2008 my life had turned into a nonstop party; I slept during the day and drank my balls off at night. I was running the most kick-ass dive bar on Rivington Street in the Lower East Side, the last neighborhood in the world with some real fucking rockers—guys who wear their hair past their shoulders, and lace-up leather pants—and I was making a good living selling the two things I loved most: Black Sabbath and cheap Budweiser.

For a while there, I was on top of the world. My buddies and I all had three things in common: We loved booze, we loved Rock 'N' Roll, and we were on a never-ending search for a good fucking time. None of us were actually married, but we called the ones we loved "our wives." As for our *girlfriends*, well, they didn't have names. (It's like I always say: If you're not fucking her, she's not your girlfriend. But if you're not fucking her, she's still your wife.) We called ourselves the Rivington Rebels, and every day was like a Rock 'N' Roll "Choose Your Own Adventure" story—we never knew where the night might take us, but it always had an interesting ending. There was just one problem: the years of drinking my face off were suddenly starting to catch up to me. I was living my life somewhere between drunk and hungover at all times. I was out of shape, overweight, feeling like shit, and popping Ibuprofen every hour just to make it through the day. The more fun I had at night, it seemed, the more I hated myself in the morning.

PASSED OUT ON THE SIDEWALK.

I remember one of my boys' birthday parties in particular. We all met up and decided to do Irish Car Bombs at every single bar we went to. (Irish Car Bombs are not something we would ever drink, which is exactly why we decided to drink them. It was my friend's birthday, after all.) We knew every bartender in NYC worth knowing, so we didn't have to pay for a damn thing, anyway—although being the classy dudes we were, we always left a big enough tip to take care of all the drinks and the toilet paper we used, so don't give us a fucking hard time if you want us to come back. Sometime after three A.M., the birthday boy and I decided to do "One Bourbon, One Scotch, and One Beer," just like the John Lee Hooker/George Thorogood song. We took both shots right in a row, then chugged the beers. Needless to say, this night ended in disaster.

The last thing I remember was being roused by two police officers, shaking me awake in the middle of the street. I was literally lying on my back in the middle of a busy road, and had no idea why. One of them poked me and said, "Hey, kid, where do you live?" I sat up, looked around, and saw my front door. Somehow, I had made it all the way back to Brooklyn, but had passed out on the pavement outside my apartment.

"I live right there," I said. "How the fuck did I end up in the street?"

"I don't know, but you better get up there and sleep it off," said the officer. It was a miracle he didn't arrest me on the spot.

I don't remember this either, but apparently I stumbled inside, called my girlfriend (who was out of town), and put the phone down while I threw up for ten minutes. It's when you don't remember things like throwing up—on a regular basis—that you realize, *maybe it's time to reevaluate my life.*

For a normal person, this would have been enough to scare them sober. But, really, what the fuck is *normal?* I went out and got drunk again the very next night, just as I always had. I just didn't give a fuck. I was a "Whiskey Rock-a-Roller" and I didn't think anything could stop me. Looking back, I know now that I got lucky. I got lucky several times a week. All the alcohol poisonings, all the I-don't-know-how-I-got-homes, were starting to add up. I kept thinking about that line in *Stripes* when Harold Ramis bets Bill Murray three dollars that he can't do five push-ups. Bill Murray barely gets himself off the ground. "I gotta get in shape," he says. "I gotta dry out or I'll be dead before I'm thirty."

On top of everything, this was right around the time that

my grandfather passed away (and I got shit-drunk at his funeral), which made me take stock of my family history. By the time he turned fifty-eight, my grandfather had already had three heart attacks and a quadruple bypass; nearly all the other men in his family had heart attacks in their fifties. My *other* grandfather had already died of a stroke, brought on by drinking and smoking. He was such a die-hard smoker, in fact, that he used to rip the filters off his cigarettes. (When I was ten, I asked him why. Here's exactly what he told me: "Because when I was your age, kid, only pussies smoked filtered cigarettes.") His wife, my stepgrandmother (not only was Grandpop a partier, he was also a ladies' man), had half a lung removed, but she still lit up a cigarette as soon as she got out of the hospital—she walked out of there with an oxygen tank on a pushcart in one hand and a cigarette in the other. My father was also a hard-partying son of a bitch—at least, until he had children. Luckily, he had a good woman around to get him to quit most of his bad habits.

At the time, I did not. My love life was a fucking mess (my girlfriend had had just about enough of my bullshit), my apartment was a mess, my body was fat and bloated, and my brain was like a fucking circus packed with tigers and trapeze artists; the only way to get them to stop doing tricks was to lobotomize myself with a bottle of whiskey. All of my friends were addicts, but I had been justifying my lifestyle with the fact that they were *bigger* addicts than I was. Everyone around me was doing cocaine, smoking weed, popping painkillers, and sleeping with random women on a daily basis. Since I mostly stuck to the legal drugs—booze and cigarettes—I honestly felt like the Goody Two-shoes of the group. (Also, I've never been a cheater. Unlike the other

Rebels, women were never on my list of vices.) I just had no idea that there was an entire world out there filled with happy, healthy people living "normal" lives without drugs or alcohol. Even when I did normal-people things, like go to the movies, I'd still smoke a joint and sneak in a six-pack.

Aside from all the partying, I hadn't realized how bad my diet was. Every night I would come home shit-drunk and eat a cheese-steak sandwich. Every morning I would wake up next to an empty beer bottle with a ciga-rette butt in the bottom of it, get on the phone and order greasy food from the diner, and go back to sleep until it was time to go to work. It didn't even cross my mind that I was un-healthy. I just didn't know that there were things to eat other than fried foods and red meat. Hell, I didn't even know what *red*

MY BROTHER, ANDY, AND ME, AT MY FATTEST.

ME AND THE DIRT, FISHING. CHECK OUT THE DOUBLEFISTING: BEER IN ONE HAND, WHISKEY IN THE OTHER...

meat was. (I thought it meant raw hamburger, because when meat is raw, it's red. But since I was only eating my hamburg-ers cooked, that meant I was just eating regular meat, right?) At the risk of sounding like a complete dumbass, I think this happens all too often in the life of a bachelor. Or maybe just in the lives of Americans in general. We get into the habit of eating certain foods—many of which we didn't even know were high in saturated fat or cholesterol or sodium; I mean, what the fuck is saturated fat anyway?—and we stick with those foods for the rest of our lives.

I did some math: The average adult gains one pound per year until death. I had about sixty years to go, but I was already forty pounds overweight, which meant I was going to die with 100+ extra pounds hanging off my ass. (Though at that size, I probably only had another thirty or forty years left anyway.) All of my boys ate the same shitty foods that I did, but all of my boys were *addicts*—I didn't realize the drugs were what was keeping them skinny. I seemed to be the only one of my friends who wasn't happy with his body, and it pissed me off. I wanted to be sexy. I wanted to be able to walk around feeling comfortable in my own skin, and not be embarrassed to take my shirt off. I didn't love myself as much as I wanted to do. The unhappier I became, the more I drank to numb the pain.

And then something happened that pushed me over the edge: my girlfriend left me. She said she couldn't sit around watching me be miserable anymore, so she packed her shit and moved out West to pursue her dreams. At first, I hated her for it. I thought, *Fuck her if she wants to leave*. It took me about a week to realize that she was right. I *was* fucking miserable, and it wasn't her fault. It was my fault for being a drunk asshole. I would have left me, too.

What I hadn't realized—for damn near twenty-eight years—is that I had been battling an addiction of my own. (I mean other than my addiction to booze and cigarettes, of course.) Because being overweight and eating like shit is an addiction, too, and it can be as hard to break as a heroin habit. I know, because in my line of work, I've watched a number of friends fall off the deep end with drugs. How they got clean is always the same story: they had to hit rock bottom.

My friend Kirk, a bass player and fellow long-hair, got pulled over while driving home to Pittsburgh to visit his mother . . . with an 8-ball of cocaine on him. The cops never found it—he'd hidden it in the waistband of his pants—but they did find the empty bag he had stashed in the cup holder of his van. (God, I loved that van. Her name was Michelle, and she was a big GMC conversion van with all-black leather interior, a fold-down bed, and a full bar in the back. I spent many nights cruising from bar to bar in that van, curled up on the bed with a girl, smoking a joint and listening to Humble Pie.) Anyway, when the cops found the baggie, they arrested Kirk. Somehow, he managed to get the 8-ball out of his waistband and swallow it before arriving at the precinct, so they just charged him with paraphernalia and released him the next morning. Unfortunately, he had to go straight to the hospital to have his stomach pumped. When they finally discharged him a week later, he went straight to Narcotics Anonymous and he's been clean ever since.

My buddy Johnny had a coke problem. He'd bounce in and out of rehab to make his family happy, but then he'd be right back at it. His signature move was to get so incredibly trashed that he'd get lost while attempting to drive himself to an after-party. He'd be so out of it that he'd park his car, hail a cab, tell the driver where he thought he was trying to go, and then to-tally forget where he left his car. Like clockwork, the cops would call the next day to tell him that his car had been im-pounded. It took losing his job, his apartment, his wife, and practically his mind before he decided to get clean. (He also had to move back home to get away from everything in the city that reminded him of his old life as an addict.)

You have to hit rock bottom in order to have the motivation and the willpower it takes to change—whether it's a health problem when you're fifty-five, or court-appointed rehab when you're twenty-five—and the breakup with my girlfriend was my rock bottom. I was finally ready to lose the weight, and I was ready to get my life back. I was going to dedicate myself to becoming the healthiest, sexiest, most delightful asshole on the planet.

This, however, would prove to be more difficult than I had imagined. I spent a month trying to come up with a plan, but came up empty. I decided that if I wanted to do something that I knew nothing about, I needed to educate myself. So I went to the health and fitness section at the bookstore, and I read book after book, all of which were written by doctors and other assholes, all of which pissed me off. *The Abs Diet*, *The Big Breakfast Diet*, *The I Diet*, *The Scarsdale Diet*, *The South Beach Diet*, *The Atkins Diet*, *The New Atkins Diet*, *The Atkins for a New You Diet*, and—get this—the fucking *Cookie Diet*. That's what really set me off. When I found out that there was a book called *The Cookie Diet*, I lost it. In my line of work, it's nearly impossible to stay healthy. My schedule alone is enough to drive anyone crazy—never seeing the sun, surrounded by drunk people. I sure as hell wasn't ready to quit drinking, but all these books were saying the same thing: you can't drink alcohol if you want to lose weight. I can't drink, but there's something on the shelf called *The Cookie Diet*? Fuck you.

That's when I decided to lose weight and get sexy my own way, to tell my own story, and to name that story *The Drunk Diet*—just to shove it up all those doctors' asses. I wasn't going to tell people how they *should* do it; I wanted to tell people how I did it. After all, I'm just a regular guy who decided to change his life around. I'm not a fucking yoga instructor, or a nutritionist (whatever the fuck that is), or an Olympic gold medalist. I'm a bartender, a *real person*. Some people are born with perfect bodies. I was not. I wanted to inspire people just like me.

One day I sat down at my computer with a bottle of wine and started typing, and I didn't stop for a year and a half. I also started telling people that I was writing a book. (I figured if I told a few people, the dream would come true. Everyone that knows me knows that I don't fuck around—if I say I'm going to write a book, I'm going to write a fucking book. And write a book, I did.) If I wasn't at work, I was at the gym or outside running. If I wasn't at work, working out, or running, I was in my square little room that I call home, typing away, telling my story about getting drunk at work and then running nine miles the next morning. Little by little, I was getting in shape, losing weight, and getting another tiny piece of my life back.

On a chilly morning in December, the day of my thirtieth birthday, I ran my first full marathon—26.2 brutal fucking miles (and I did it in under four hours). And I'm here to tell you: If this fat, drunk, chain-smoking asshole can do it, so can you. This is the story of how I lost forty pounds . . . *wasted*.

WARNING: THIS BOOK WAS **NOT** WRITTEN ENTIRELY SOBER.

PART I

FRENCH FRIES AND METHADONE
OR,
LEARNING TO PUT DOWN THE KETCHUP

CHAPTER ONE

How the Fuck Did I Get Fat?

LÜC'S LAW: IF YOU DON'T LIKE IT, FIX IT.

MY FIRST DRUM SET.

grew up in a cornfield twenty miles south of Omaha, Nebraska, and I was raised by a couple of Rock 'N' Roll hell-raisers. Seriously, for their thirtieth wedding anniversary, my parents went to an Ozzy Osbourne concert. In fact, if it wasn't for my father, I'd probably be a short-haired pussy who listens to Michael Bolton. (Though, if it were up to my mother, I would have just been a girl.)

See, my mother was a hairdresser, and she worked out of a salon in the basement of our house. My father built her a separate entrance next to the garage, and every day she worked her fingers to the bone giving farmers' wives and Lutherans blowouts and perms—which is why our house always smelled like peroxide and menthol cigarettes.

I grew up in that salon. My earliest years were spent in a crib over by the sinks, and most of my childhood involved crawling up the back of a thirty-five-year-old hair dryer to take rollers out of a sixty-five-year-old, blue-haired woman's head while she read the *National Enquirer* and believed every single sordid detail of the two-headed dog story and the governor of South Dakota's surprising lack of testicles. Thinking back on it now, it's obvious where I acquired my obsession for my hair—my mother may not have been able to actually turn me into a girl, but she did a damn good job trying.

I still remember the day that I discovered Rock 'N' Roll—I was nine, and I'd had just about enough of this girl shit. I know I was nine because that's around the time that my father kept his 1989 two-tone blue Dodge Dakota parked in the driveway, directly under the basketball hoop. (The truck was about a year old, which would make the year 1990.) That particular afternoon, my dad had taken my mom's car to town and I had been shooting hoops by myself. After about five minutes, I got tired of chasing the basketball into the street after it had ricocheted off the hood of the truck, and for whatever reason, I decided to climb into the driver's seat.

My dad is a sort of jack-of-all-trades—he does all his own mechanic work, and my brother and I were usually right there with him, helping him out with the tools. So when I realized that my dad hadn't taken the keys with him—he'd left them in the ignition—I thought to myself, *I can move this fucking thing. Let's go for it!* I turned the key forward one notch, nervous about the fact that my video games would surely be taken from me if anyone ever found out that I'd started the engine. But that's when it happened: the radio started playing. And I liked what I was hearing. Actually, I *loved* what I was hearing. The first song ended and the second song began and—it took me a moment—but I figured out that they were both by the same band. *This isn't the radio*, I thought. *This is a cassette tape!* I ejected the tape, a cream-colored cassette with black writing that

MY FIRST REAL DRUM SET.

said: ZZ TOP. DEGÜELLO. At the time I didn't know which was the name of the group and which was the name of the album, and I no clue had to pronounce "Degüello," but I popped the tape back in the deck, turned up the volume, and decided to look around; I liked this music so much, I wanted more.

I didn't find any other tapes, but I did discover, underneath the driver's seat, the latest issue of *Playboy* and a bottle of peppermint schnapps. So there I was, blasting "Cheap Sunglasses" and flipping through pages of voluptuous, naked women, and I knew, right then and there, that I was hooked for life. As of that moment, I was officially a Rock 'N' Roller.

A few months later, when I turned ten, my parents took me to school band orientation. (My folks were big on extracurricular activities, and playing in the band was one of them.) I had originally planned to go with the trombone, but ZZ Top didn't have a trombone player. So I decided to play the drums. Unfortunately, I had to learn to play the xylophone first, before they let me play the snare drum, because they wanted to teach us about melodies and how to read music. What a bunch of horseshit. The xylophone is like a fucking keyboard that doesn't plug in. *If I had wanted to learn to play the piano,* I thought, *I would have picked out the goddamn piano.* And as it turned out, I wasn't a damn bit good at the xylophone, but I did turn out to be one hell of a drummer (just not right away).

My first band was called Flux. I was in the seventh grade, and we played Metallica cover songs at the local church. We booked our first gig before we even had a singer, so my brother sang for us—and he did the whole show holding the CD liner notes so he'd know what the lyrics were.

The next year I got serious and started a "real" band with some kids from area schools. We called ourselves 5th Street Capital (terrible name, I know), but we played our own songs, and we were pretty damn good. So good, in fact, that we signed up for a local Battle of the Bands contest that was offering a $500 grand prize. We were up against a hotshot high school group of rich-kid seniors. They were so cocky—pretty-boy dickheads whose parents had bought them all expensive guitars and amps (the boys in *my* band all had to earn our gear by working after-school jobs), but we kicked their sorry asses. Before long, we were getting calls to play gigs all over town.

By the time I was fifteen, we'd booked a job at the hottest Rock 'N' Roll spot in Omaha—The Ranch Bowl, a dingy little 400-seat club sandwiched in the back of a bowling alley. Over the years, I'd seen all kinds of bands play there—Pearl Jam, Slipknot, 2 Skinnee J's (I saw them fourteen times, actually), the Urge, 311, the Nixons—all kinds of groups that I eventually stopped listening to. As a teenager growing up in a small town, I'd been awestruck by the big-name bands that rolled through there every weekend; now here I was playing a gig at the same club, before I was even old enough to drive myself there.

5th Street Capital lasted a whole year and a half. The singer was kind of a prima donna asshole, and frankly, so was I. He had gone off to college and commuted to practice for a few months, but all we did was fight, so we eventually called it quits. After that, I decided I was ready for the big leagues. I posted my résumé in every guitar shop and drum store in town and ended up joining a band with a bunch of dudes twice my age. I was seventeen years old, and my bass player was a cable guy by day with a wife and a kid to feed. The music was god-awful, but I didn't give a shit as long as I got to play the drums.

TOO MUCH OF A GOOD THING

Right up until I turned eighteen, I was a pretty straitlaced kid and never got into much trouble. For the most part, if I wasn't at school, I was at home playing the drums. In fact, the only reason I *went* to high school was because the band rehearsed during first period. If it had been math or chemistry, go fuck yourself. I would have just stayed home. Things changed, however, when I got to college. I was "studying" music at the local university but all they were teaching me was a bunch of bullshit about classical music and playing the piano. I wanted to play Rock 'N' Roll and break shit. Basically, I was bored. And with all that idle time—time that should have been spent studying musical theory—I discovered a new love: beer. (When it comes to alcohol, yes, I was a bit of a late bloomer.)

You might say that I was destined to develop a love of the bottle—it's in my blood. My great-great-great-grandfather, Louis Hanson, was friends with the greatest beer-makers of all time: Eberhard Anheuser, and Anhesuer's son-in-law, Adol-

MOM, ANDY, THE KING OF BEERS, AND ME.

phus Busch. Actually, Hanson and Anheuser came over from Germany on the same boat, back in 1860. My great-great-great-grandfather eventually settled in Omaha, Nebraska, and opened a bar called Hanson's Saloon. Meanwhile, Anheuser bought a struggling brewery in St. Louis, Missouri. A few years later, after Anheuser-Busch became the first U.S. brewer to use pasteurization to keep beer fresh (and after pioneering the use of the refrigerated railroad car), Hanson's Saloon became the first bar outside of St. Louis to sell Budweiser beer. My family takes their beer so seriously, in fact, that my parents named their first-born—my brother—Andrew Adolph Carl, in honor of Adolphus Busch.

I can still remember the very first time I got drunk. I was a freshman in college, I'd just turned eighteen, and I had convinced my brother Andy to buy me two six-packs of beer. Then I called up the hottest girl I knew. Her name was Lacy (no, she wasn't a stripper . . . although her best friend was), and she had a white Corvette with red leather interior. We sat in the parking lot drinking warm beers until we were shit-drunk. I felt like such a badass, sitting in that hot car with a hot chick, drinking beers that my brother had bought for me. Within weeks, however, I decided that I didn't want to rely on my brother for my beer anymore. So, I took his birth certificate and social security card to the DMV and told them I had lost my driver's license. We lived in such a Podunk town that the DMV didn't even have computers yet. Ten minutes later, I had a genuine Nebraska ID, with my brother's name, date of birth (he's two and a half years older than me), and my fucking picture! Before long I had graduated to drinking beer every night, and eating crap like Chef Boyardee and fried chicken every day. In a matter of months, I'd packed almost thirty pounds on to my formerly 165-pound frame.

With my new love of beer came a new love of partying. Unfortunately, my roommates were total squares—one was a computer nerd, one was a Bible-beater, and one was an openly gay virgin who loved to masturbate in the bathtub. (I know this not because I was in there with him, but because I could hear the water whooshing around like a violent, seven-minute-long tidal wave every time he took a bath.) One night I was drinking beers with my roommates, who didn't drink, which would make me the only person getting drunk, which was boring as hell. I'd heard about a party at some girl's house, so I talked my Bible-beater roommate into driving me over there, in my car. (I might have been a drunk, but I was a safe drunk.)

The "party" ended up being just a group of eighteen- and nineteen-year-olds living on their own for the first time, learning how to drink. It was exactly like parties in high school, except that if you had a beer in your hand, it meant you might get laid.

(Actually, that probably happened at high school parties, too, I just didn't go to them.) I was sitting on the couch, next to my lame roommate and his equally lame girlfriend, staring off into space, when I noticed another guy sitting all alone, beer in hand. This was right around the time I'd started growing my hair long—it was just below my ears and wasn't sure what it was doing with itself yet. This guy had a similar hair-vibe going on, and I liked it. Most of all I liked the fact that he was sitting on a case of Budweisers, so I went right over. "Hey, dude," I said, "I heard there's another party at my dorm, and I think there are better looking chicks there. Want to come with me?"

"This party sucks," he said. "And I have more beer in my trunk."

This guy, Ryan, would become my bandmate for the next two years (I was forming a group with some dudes a little closer to my own age; we called ourselves Smith Victer), and my best friend for the rest of my life. Together, we quickly gained a reputation for throwing the best parties on campus, right in my fucking dorm room—a major accomplishment considering that I lived right above the dorm Nazi, the asshole in charge of making sure the campus stayed dry. (Still, my fridge was stocked with beer, and I always had a bottle of booze stashed underneath my bed.)

Back then, my uncle had a piece-of-shit van that was only firing on five of its six cylinders, and he said that if I was willing the pay the insurance, I could have it for free. *Fuck yeah!* We cleaned that fucker out, painted our new band's logo on the back window, built seats, and carpeted the whole thing. I also erected a wooden wall separating the front seat from the back end so we'd have a place to store our gear (and, of course, the booze), and I cut a little carpeted flap in it that could be flipped up or down, depending. This came in handy whenever we got pulled over with underage girls—you couldn't see through to the back from the driver's seat, unless you knew about the secret flap. The hard part was getting drunk nineteen-year-olds to shut the fuck up long enough for the cops to write me a ticket for a busted taillight, or whatever the problem was that day.

By the end of freshman year, I'd been caught with alcohol on eight separate occasions, so they threw me out of the dorms. (The official rule was that you'd be thrown out after getting caught three times, but I was a smooth talker.) They also told me I had to go to on-campus AA meetings but, of course, I didn't go. I didn't even show up for class, why the fuck would I go to a drinking meeting? By the time I was registering for my fourth year of school, I found myself signing up for classes that I'd already failed three times. So I basically said, fuck it. I wanted to move to the big city and play music for a living, anyway. I was living in a town with three churches and no stoplights, with no real culture other than "white." The only thing I wanted to do was get out. I didn't know where I was going, or who I would meet, or what I would see, and I didn't give a shit. I wanted out of a world that seemed created to keep you in. I was a mailman's son, who was destined to become a mailman, too, and have three children and a mortgage before I hit thirty. It's not that I was opposed to that kind of life—my family seems quite happy, as far as families go, and I consider myself lucky. It's that I wanted to see what else was out there before giving in to what had been appointed to me by the cornfields of my youth.

I'd heard about a local band from the nearby town of Lincoln, Nebraska, that had moved to New York City. I'd never met any of them, and it's not worth mentioning the name of the group (because you've never heard of them), but I tracked them down on the Internet and sent them an e-mail. (This was way before MySpace and Facebook and Twitter and whatever is about to come next.) As it turned out, the band was on tour and would be playing a final show in their hometown, about forty minutes away from my home outside of Omaha, before heading back to New York. Not only could I thumb a ride to New York after the show, they said, but they also had a room for rent in their Brooklyn apartment! *Fuck, yeah*! I met my new roommates after their show, and we all crashed on a friend's floor for the night. The next morning, after downing a couple of beers, we were off to NYC. In one week, I had quit school, sold my only possession (my car), quit my band, and said good-bye to my mother. I hopped in a big blue van with two guys I didn't really know, and left the Midwest for the first time in my life.

OFF TO THE BIG CITY

We arrived in Brooklyn at five A.M. I was so exhausted from the drive that I slept that entire first day. The next day I went to Manny's Music on Forty-eighth Street and applied for a job. (One of my new roommates worked at Rudy's, a horn shop across the street from Manny's, so I tagged along when he went to work, since I had no idea how to get anywhere.) I had two years' experience selling drums back home, so they gave me the job on the spot. I'd be working forty-eight hours a week for $226, after taxes. Since my share of the rent was $575 a month, that didn't leave much left over for my partying habits—or a healthy meal, for that matter.

Although I made friends, at first, I didn't meet any other Rock 'N' Rollers. That, mixed with the extreme life change, made me feel like an outcast. I don't know why I gave a fuck, it's not like there are a shitload of rockers in Nebraska, but I was sure that everyone was looking at me, with my shoulder-length hair and tight black jeans, like I was a total freak. I sort of assumed that the legendary rock culture of NYC—bands like the New York Dolls and clubs like CBGB—had been taken over by Starbucks and Subway, and that I'd never really fit in. All I knew was that I was living in an all-black neighborhood in Brooklyn, working in an all-tourist neighborhood in Midtown, and quickly losing my mind. Everywhere I looked I saw either rich people in suits or people from the projects. I was completely overwhelmed, and decided that the best way to deal with that was to *make* myself fit in. So I went into the bathroom with a pair of scissors and chopped off my most prized possession: my hair. I regretted this instantly. I spent the next two hours drinking 40s on the front stoop, looking at pictures of myself with long hair, and spent the next two years growing it back.

Eventually, I met a couple guys that I'd become inseparable from over the next few years—Dino Casino and Dirt Bag (or "the Dirt," for short). Dino worked in the guitar department. I gave him the nickname "Dino Casino" because I didn't like his real name and, to me, he looked like a Dino Casino. Dirt Bag was a customer at the shop, a troubled, confused dude who worked in film editing. I gave him the name "Dirt Bag" because when it came to women, well, he was a dirt bag. The Dirt was taking lessons at the same drum school as one of my other co-workers. One day, he came in the shop on his way to lunch, and Dino and the Dirt and I all ended up eating together. Finally, I had found some drinking buddies.

Within a few months, I even found some guys that needed a drummer. I didn't really dig the music they were playing and we had absolutely nothing in common, but at this point, I would have done anything to be able to play drums with anyone. I felt like such an outcast that I was convinced no other band would have me. We got along OK, even though the other guys didn't drink and they were a bunch of rich kids from Connecticut, but they had a rehearsal studio, which meant I now had a place to store my drum kit. I called my father and asked him to ship out my drums as soon as possible.

Every night after work, the Dirt and I went to a scummy dive bar called the Village Idiot on Fourteenth Street and Eighth Avenue. (Don't look for it now; it's not there anymore.) The Idiot had five-dollar pitchers of Busch, a jukebox packed with old country songs, and smelled strongly of vomit and urine. It was the only place where I could afford to get drunk, and at this point in my short NYC career, the only place I felt at home. There were never really any classy ladies there, though, mostly just a bunch of drunk assholes, hitting on the one random girl with enough guts to push her way past flying bar stools and the smell of piss. I'd drink until they threw me out—every single night—then take the train home, sleep four hours, order a bacon-egg-and-cheese, and head back up to Manny's and do it all over again.

After six months of this routine, my roommates decided that they couldn't handle my constant partying. So they left me a note:

> *The lease is up the first of the month.*
> *We're getting a two-bedroom.*
> *You're too crazy.*
> *We can't live with you anymore.*

(From that moment on, I've had a "no note" rule with all of my roommates. Just say it to my face, you fucking pussy.) I moved in with one of the guys from work. A few weeks later,

HOW THE FUCK DID I GET FAT?

he came home with some news. "Listen," he said, "I caught wind that they're going to fire you because you don't sell enough drums."

I took offense at this for two reasons: (1) because no matter what job I've ever had, I always work my ass off, and (2) because it's fucking Manhattan. Who the fuck buys *drums?* I don't know a single person whose apartment is big enough for a drum set, let alone anyone who is willing to piss off all the neighbors with the noise. Needless to say, I didn't show up for work the next day. (*You think you can fire me? Fuck you. I quit.*) Instead, I got on the train at eight A.M., went to Queens—my first time ever in Queens—and got a job in the drum department at Guitar Center. A few months later, I read that Manny's got rid of the drum department. A few years after that, they went out of business. I guess I wasn't the only one who wasn't selling enough drums.

The Guitar Center job sucked hard. It was an hour-and-twenty-minute commute—each way—for a six-dollar-an-hour gig. After two weeks, I called up the manager and told him that my band had a record deal. Sure, I lied. But that job could go fuck itself.

I was walking around the East Village a few days later, looking for a job, when I saw a HELP WANTED sign posted in the window of a fast-food, after-hours Mexican joint. I walked in, and after a quick chat the manager called my (only) reference . . . which was actually my brother, Andy. (I lied on my application and said that I'd worked at an Olive Garden in Los Angeles. Andy, who was living in L.A. at the time, knew that if he got any phone calls from a New York number, he was supposed to pick up and say, "Olive Garden, how can I help you?") My brother told this guy that I was the best damn employee he'd ever had, and that he wished I'd move back to L.A. and work for him again. I got the job.

Now I was working five nights a week, making about eighty bucks a night (or $400 a week). After making $226 a week at Manny's, I thought I was rich. The job itself kind of sucked, though—we were open until five A.M., an hour later than the bars, so people would come in completely trashed after a night of drinking, pissed that they hadn't gotten laid, and sometimes take it out on the guy behind the counter serving tacos (me). My *other* duties, besides serving tacos, included cleaning

DRINKING AT THE TACO SHOP.

up after the fights—and when you work at a shitty after-hours spot, you see a lot of them. One night, I watched a dude break another dude's nose because he didn't like the way the guy had talked to his girl. Then, the guy with the broken nose picked himself off the floor and hawked a blood-soaked loogie directly into the other dude's face. (I saw this guy around the neighborhood for years after that, and had to kick him out of the taco shop almost every night. Cocaine is a hell of a drug.) From time to time, I even cleaned up blood from people shooting up in the bathroom. I used rubber gloves and bleach but, quite frankly, I didn't give a shit. I'd get drunk every night with the Mexicans, listening to Slayer and KISS. Occasionally, I'd even convince a girl to go out with me. Of course, I also had access to all-you-can-eat tacos every day, from the hours of eleven P.M. to five A.M. Perks!

After six months of selling tacos, partying it up in New York, and playing Rock 'N' Roll, my band booked a three-month tour. *Fuck, yeah!* I quit my job at the taco shop, moved out of my apartment, and used every penny I had to book a flight to visit my brother before we were set to travel the country. Andy and I partied it up in L.A. for a few days and then decided to head down to Mexico with our buddies Royce and "the Meat." Four Nebraskan corn-fed hell-raisers—all of us over six feet tall—packed in a Geo Metro with a bottle of whiskey; it was a recipe for disaster. The bottle was empty before we even reached the border.

About an hour south, we found a big outdoor bar—actually it was a two-level arena with a beach volleyball pit in the middle—and made ourselves at home. By this point, we were all pretty shitty, and it made complete sense to my drunk-ass brother that, since I sold tacos for a living, I also spoke Spanish. In reality, I only knew about forty words and thirty of them would only get us into more trouble. I went to every bouncer on the way out and asked if he could tell me where to find the "donkey show." After being laughed out of the club, we decided to head to another town to try and find this woman who gets fucked by a horse.

We ended up on Revolution Street in Tijuana. We parked the car at the end of the strip, walked into the first strip club we saw, and didn't stop partying until they kicked us out of the last strip club. That's when my brother and I went to take a piss.

"Dude," my brother slurred at me, "we're sneaking this stripper over the border in the trunk. Tell her to meet us at the car when she gets off."

"You've got to be fucking kidding me," I said.

"No, man. I like this chick. Let's take her to America where she can make some *real* money."

"Listen, fucker," I told him, "even if I knew how to say that shit in Spanish, there's no way in hell I'd do it."

Five minutes later, I was doing my best to tell her where we were parked. Meanwhile, the lights in the club had come on and three Mexicans were asking us if we wanted to go to an after-hours place. *"Fuck, yeah!"* we said. (The stripper was later escorted out of the club by two security guards, both of whom I had asked to tell me where I could find the donkey show. I guess they didn't trust us to leave her the hell alone.)

We followed the guys to the "after-hours club," which was actually nothing more than a tip-off to the cops that four drunk gringos were driving down the road, and we were pulled over within blocks. My brother rolled down his window and confessed, "Listen, I'm fucking wasted. I'm not going to pass any sobriety tests."

The cops pulled him out of the car and tried to get him to walk a straight line anyway. Royce and I were shitting our pants, and somehow the Meat even managed to call the American consulate. We were not the least bit interested in spending time in a Mexican prison. In desperation, I told my brother to offer the cops a bribe.

"How much?"

"Thirty dollars," said the officer.

My brother told them he only had twenty bucks left, and the cops agreed to the price. I don't know who was more stupid, my brother for trying to barter with the cops, or the cops for believing him. And then Andy pulled a fifty-dollar bill from his pocket. The price had just gone up, but at that point, we didn't give a shit. We headed back to the border with no money and no stripper in the trunk—which was a good thing, because Border Security searched our car—and we never got to see that woman get fucked by a horse.

After a week in California, I'd had enough. When I got back to New York, however, the band informed me that the tour had been cancelled. I was pissed. I'd given up my job and my apartment, and I had absolutely no money. (Rich kids from Connecticut have no concept of what it's like to be broke.) So I called up Dino and asked if I could crash on his floor until I found an apartment. I needed a job, too, so I went back to the taco shop—and just as I was walking up, the owner was hanging that NOW HIRING sign in the window. "Take that sign down, baby," I said. "I'm back, and I'm broke."

Dino, it turns out, was actually crashing on his friend Mikey's couch in an apartment on Bleeker Street, so in the beginning, I slept on the floor, Dino on the couch, and Mikey on the bed on a loft overhanging the kitchen. Before long, however, we all moved in with Dan, our next-door neighbor. Dan was a full-time student, and he spent most weekends at his girlfriend's house on Long Island, which is why Mikey decided that he could live in Dan's apartment and just not tell his parents that he'd moved; that way he could spend half the rent money his parents gave him on the shared apartment, and the other half on booze and drugs. It was the same basic layout—living room, kitchen, and loft—only this apartment also had a separate bedroom, so Mikey took the bedroom, and

Dino and I slept in the living room. We did have one rule though: whoever brought home a chick got dibs on the bedroom. (Dan was not made aware of this arrangement.) If Mikey got the room, however, we never knew what to expect, because Mikey was a bisexual (we called him Bi-key) as well as a total freak. You never knew who or what might be walking out of that bedroom in the morning.

Around the same time, Dino started getting a little more serious with his girlfriend, and the apartment was getting too damn crowded. Some nights I even slept in my band's rehearsal studio. There was only one problem with that arrangement: our bass player was spending some nights in the rehearsal studio, too—along with his transsexual prostitute girlfriend who didn't speak English. (The first time we met her, in fact, Dirt Bag screamed out, "That's a dude!" I kicked his ass for being so rude. It wasn't until later that I found out he was technically correct—she *was* a dude. But he still deserved the ass-beating.) My bass player had met this girl (or guy) on Craigslist, and found out that she and her roommate both turned tricks in their apartment. So whenever her roommate had a client, they slept at the studio. Since I sure as hell wasn't going to sleep in the studio with *those* two, I learned to call ahead; and basically, where I was sleeping at night depended on whether or not my bass player's girlfriend's roommate was getting paid for sex. But I didn't really care. I brought home tacos after work to keep the boys happy. We were just a few broke kids with nothing to lose.

Eventually, my band finished recording our record and it was actually about to come out on a fairly major label. I was out celebrating with the Dirt, when I ran into another drummer from a band that we sometimes jammed with. "What happened, bro?" he asked me. "I heard you're not in the band anymore?" Apparently, someone in my band had called and asked if he knew any drummers. I went into the bathroom of the bar and called up the kids from Connecticut and let them have it. *I quit my job and gave up my apartment for you fucks, and this is the thanks I get?* I was in there yelling for so long that the Dirt thought I had passed out, so he broke down the door to make sure I was all right. I found out that they'd hired some asshole to re-record everything I'd done, note for note, except for two tracks. I was paid a thousand dollars for those two songs—the most money I'd ever seen at one time—so I got on Craigslist and decided to take the first apartment I looked at, a small one-bedroom in Brooklyn. (I wrote most of this book in that apartment. I still live there to this day.) At least I didn't have to sleep in the studio anymore.

DROWNING MY SORROWS IN A SANDWICH

So far, the big city was beating the shit out of me. I'd been kicked out of my band, I wasn't happy with my reputation as the "heavy metal taco guy," and I was struggling to pay rent in a town where everyone else my age was living off their parents. That's around the time I started drowning my sorrows in food.

There is a certain twenty-four-hour deli on the Lower East Side that I started going to nearly every night. I'd stumble in, drunk, usually on my way home from work at the taco shop, and grab a sandwich before getting on the subway to Brooklyn. (You can only eat so many tacos.) In fact, I went there on so many drunk nights, ordering that same fucking sandwich, that they named the son of a bitch after me. It's called the Borracho, which is Spanish for drunk.

The Borracho is hero bread with hot roast beef, melted cheddar, tomatoes, pickles, mayo, black pepper, and BBQ sauce, and it's a drunk asshole's dream-come-true at four in the morning. I'd top that off with a bag of Cheetos, a Diet Dr Pepper, a couple of Budweiser tallboys, and ten dollars' worth of scratch-off lottery tickets. I'd go home to my big-ass TV and put on my favorite show, *M*A*S*H*, and I'd eat my sandwich, drink my beer, and scratch lottery tickets until I passed out. Even after all that junk, when I woke up in the morning the first thing on my mind was a cheeseburger. I'd been getting my ass kicked all over New York for the last four years by then, and it was really starting to show; I was even fatter than I was in college. Plus I was bloated, and I was only taking a shit every other day—if I was lucky. If there's one thing I've learned from losing weight, it's that you can't be truly happy if you're constipated. I felt like I had about thirteen dead hamsters in my colon, on a near daily basis. How the fuck could you expect me to have a smile on my face?

But then good things started to happen: I was out drinking my face off one night, when I ran into a party promoter I'd met—just like every other rocker in this fucking town—at the taco shop. Georgie was huge in the New York party scene, as well as one of the guys in charge of the biggest, baddest Rock 'N' Roll party in town, the "Motherfucker." The fact that he was even talking to me was a big deal. He told me he was opening a new club in the neighborhood and asked me to come work for him. *Fuck, yeah!*

Okay, so that job only lasted about two weeks. (The higher-up owners were kind of a bunch of pricks, and we caught wind that they were looking to fire five other bartenders who had been working their asses off, which didn't sit right with me.) I found out about another new club opening down the street, with live bands playing every night, and decided to jump ship. I worked there from the day it opened to the day it closed, about two years later. And before long, another friend called me up with another po-

tential job, so I interviewed to work at a kick-ass dive bar in the neighborhood—called Welcome to the Johnson's—for a happy hour shift on Thursdays.

ME AND THE DIRT AT WELCOME TO THE JOHNSON'S, BACK IN ITS HEYDAY.

Suddenly I had three jobs: taco shop, big club with live bands, and the dive bar—but the dive was my favorite. I could do my own thing and play my own music and, since my friends loved to hang out and spend their money, my boss loved me. After just a few months, in fact, my boss told me she was opening a new bar down the street—St. Jerome's—and asked if I would come by and check it out.

BARTENDING AT THE JOHNSON'S, I HID MY FAT WELL.

I went in on the night it opened. It was a Thursday, after my happy hour shift, and it was empty. I knew I would never hang out in there. It was too bright, the music sucked, and the bartender was bald. I schmoozed for an hour and left. But when my boss called a week later and asked if I could fill in the following Sunday night, I said *Fuck, yeah!* (I never turned down a

shift of any kind. You need a door guy? Call me. You need someone to clean the toilets? Call me.) I met up with a DJ friend of
mine, Johnny, and we planned the party to end all parties.
When Sunday rolled around, we absolutely *killed* it. We had
managed to pack a bar that no one had ever heard of—on a
fucking Sunday night. The very next day, the boss called.
"Pick any night of the week," she said, "and it's your night."
From that day on, the place was known as Lüc's bar.

For the first time, I felt like I belonged in New York. My
buddies and I were playing great Rock 'N' Roll at a time when
no other bars in the city were, and our friends would spend
their nights running up and down Rivington Street, raising
all kinds of hell. I finally quit the taco shop for good, after
nearly four years. I just didn't need it anymore. (Though every
now and then I would still hear, "Hey, aren't you the taco
guy?") And before long I got yet another call from the boss.
She knew how much I loved St. Jerome's, and how hard I had
been working, so she offered me the chance to take over
management. I couldn't believe it! But when she first sat me
down and asked me, I actually said no. I didn't really want
the responsibility. Plus, I had joined a new band—shortly after
getting kicked out of my old one—and I wanted to be able to
leave town whenever we booked a gig. I wasn't ready to give
up on my dream of being a rock star. And I sure as hell didn't
want to be "the boss." Nobody likes his boss. Bosses are usually
assholes. When she asked me to take some time to think
things over, though, I agreed.

After a few days of soul searching, I decided to take the job.
After all, a buck is a buck, and I didn't have any. Taking over
the bar eventually meant that I didn't have enough time to
play in the band anymore, which had been one of my biggest
fears. But I'm a firm believer in the notion that everything

happens for a reason. Every band I had ever been in fell to shit, and this one turned out to be no different—the lead singer went off to do a fucking reality TV show, which just goes against everything I fucking believe in. And these days, he wears his hear short and is back in school to get a Masters degree. Gradually, playing the drums became more of a social thing rather than a way to make money. And I was okay with

PLAYING (AND DRINKING).

that. I was making way more money than I ever had, bartending two nights a week at the Johnson's, and hosting a party every Friday night at *my* bar. My bar! I was finally *somebody.* Somebody who could afford to pay his phone bill.

Even though I had everything going for me, something still wasn't right. Being overweight was always on my mind. Growing up in the Midwest, you think it's okay to eat mashed potatoes and burritos every day. Add fifteen beers a night, seven nights a week, and you've got a guaranteed recipe for Fat City. It was ironic, then, that I had built this new life for myself in a town where the most beautiful people in the world migrate to live amongst themselves. All of my friends were gorgeous with great bodies, even though they ate as much shit as I did. I specifically remember hanging out one afternoon with Newman, that son of a bitch; I watched him eat an Italian hero for lunch, chicken nuggets and French fries later (when we went bowling), and then he went out for pasta with his wife, all while getting drunk off Budweisers all day. He does this every day, yet he remains stick thin. Some of us aren't that lucky.

To me, there comes a time when all of the "I've had enough's" and the "today is the day's" add up and you have to make a decision. Am I going to do something about this, or am I going to let it get the best of me? Every one of us comes to this crossroads, where you must choose between the easy way or the hard way. At the risk of sounding like a fucking motivational speaker, there ain't no way but the hard way. If you want something bad enough, you must earn it. If you get something handed to you, you'll never appreciate it. Some people were born with perfect bodies. I was not. But God damn it, I was determined to get one.

CHAPTER TWO

If You Love Me, You'll Stop Feeding Me

LÜC'S LAW: YOU DIDN'T GET FAT IN ONE DAY, AND YOU WILL NOT GET SEXY IN ONE DAY. OR ONE MONTH. OR ONE YEAR.

f I decide that I'm going to do something, I fucking do it. I don't just sit around talking about something that I'm going to do—I make it happen. Even when I was a kid, I said I was going to play Rock 'N' Roll and tour the country, and I did it. (I did it in a fucking minivan with a bunch of bands you've never heard of, and I slept on my bass drum, but I did it). I'd made it in New York fucking City with nothing but a dream, and became co-manager of a Rock 'N' Roll bar in the middle of Manhattan; it was time for something new. I hadn't failed at anything yet, and I sure as shit wasn't going to start now.

Unfortunately, I had a rude awakening. I soon realized that losing weight is not always so cut and dry as going on a fucking "diet." In order to understand this we must look at the big picture. Let's talk about ancient man for a minute . . .

Every person—from every part of the world—was designed to adapt to his surroundings and climate for one very specific purpose: to feed himself. People living closer to the equator were designed to be thin, lean, and quick enough to kill a fast-moving animal, like a gazelle or a cheetah. (Well, maybe not a cheetah, but whatever.) These people lived in a place with no winter and were constantly burning off calories. People in North America and Europe, however, where there *is* a winter, were designed differently. These people needed more fat cells, so they could store as much energy as possible, just in case they had to go a few days without eating. If a bad winter killed off all the buffalo, these people needed to be able to survive.

It's like the human body's version of hibernation. Much like a squirrel gathers nuts for the winter, your stomach gathers bacon fat. This is why, after centuries of evolution, "six-pack-abs" have become so desirable. They're nearly impossible to attain unless your great-great-great-great-great-great-grandfather was hunting gazelle, as opposed to cows. (There's a lot more athleticism involved in killing a fast-moving animal than there is in killing an animal that just stands there and stares at you while you poke holes in it.) What I'm saying is, the type of body you're destined to have was partially determined at birth— also, LL Cool J's kid is one lucky bastard.

People, of course, have evolved in the last few thousand years, but our fat cells haven't been so lucky. With the invention of the refrigerator, and of McDonald's, people living in colder climates no longer need to store such large amount of fats. Try telling that to your DNA.

As for me, I was raised in the Midwest by two fat parents. My mother made dinner for my father, brother, and me every night—after she had worked hard in the salon all goddamn day long—and I love her and respect her for it. But how and what you eat as an adult is something you pick up at a very young age. I still find myself calling my mother when I get a wild hair up my ass and want to cook something: "Hey, Mom, how in the hell did you make that crazy casserole?" The foods you ate grow-ing up tend to stick with you for life.

For example, I've hated lettuce my whole life. Actually, I'm not sure where in the hell I picked that up—my mom always made a small salad with dinner. My "salad," however, consisted of tomatoes, olives, carrots, and a couple of cucumbers, but it was mostly croutons smothered in French dressing. I just hated lettuce. I hated the texture. I didn't like the way it felt in my mouth when I chewed it. I didn't even like the taste, even though lettuce doesn't have much of a taste, and I refused to eat it—even on a burger. I didn't touch lettuce for the first twenty-five years of my life.

I had a similar relationship with nearly every vegetable in the supermarket. About the only vegetables I would eat were canned corn and canned green beans. Yes, *canned*. When I was a kid, my mom would open up a can of vegetables, throw it in the microwave, and put it on the dinner table. I don't know why. I didn't ask questions. That's just what we ate. My whole life, I thought fresh vegetables were gross and pretentious. (I didn't even know what the word "pretentious" meant until I moved to the big city. Just *saying* that word is pretentious where I come from.)

My mother had about eight to ten different meals that she would rotate. Most of them were chicken-based, like broiled chicken with homemade noodles or dumplings, but we also had beef Stroganoff, and Reubens, which I wouldn't touch because they had something on them that resembled lettuce. Later I learned to love them, and it became a problem.

Rounding out her list of go-to meals were Sloppy Joes, mac 'n' cheese, and steak, which we had about once a week, along-side canned green beans and baked (meaning thrown in the microwave) potatoes, covered in sautéed mushrooms and sour cream. Sometimes we had a pasta dish, like spaghetti with meat sauce or lasagna. (She made the meat sauce from scratch, using ox tails. It would sit on the stove and simmer all day long. If I'd had any idea that ox tails were in there, I wouldn't have eaten it. But damn, it was good.) She also made rice that she cooked in the oven using mushroom soup and orange juice. It sounds weird, but it's amazing.

If we had fruit with our dinner, it also came out of a can. She would often serve cottage cheese with canned peaches, with a cherry on top and a touch of mayonnaise. I remember going to the grocery store with her once. We were in the canned fruit aisle and I picked up some canned peaches. She told me to put them back. "Those are packed in syrup," she said. "They're bad for you. Get the ones packed in water." Now, at least she chose the peaches packed in water and not heavy syrup, but now that I know better, I just don't understand—there were fresh peaches two aisles over. I guess, when you're a busy working mother, you don't have time to find the perfect goddamn peach and then slice the son of a bitch up.

Thanksgiving dinner consisted of buying the biggest turkey in the grocery store and cooking it in the oven for two days. For sides, we had homemade stuffing with liver (my mother and my aunt hid the liver because they knew the kids wouldn't eat it if we knew it was in there), mashed potatoes, turkey giblet gravy, cranberry sauce, gooey white rolls, and green bean casserole, which was my favorite—canned string beans, cream of mushroom soup, and French's fried onions, just like the recipe on the side of the can. I would devour half the damn pan.

On Thanksgiving, of course, it's okay to go ahead and eat your face off and enjoy yourself. The problem with my family is that we don't eat meals like this once a year, we eat them seven nights a week. When Mom didn't have time to cook, she'd order a pizza that my dad would pick up on his way home from work. (Or we'd have KFC, Wendy's, or some other terrible fast food.) Not so long ago, I called my dad while he was eating dinner. He said Mom had called and told him to pick up some burgers on the way home because she didn't have time to cook, but by the time he got home, she had made Sloppy Joes. "You ate the burgers *and* the Sloppy Joes, didn't you?" I asked him. Of course he did.

That's just the way it was for us corn-fed Midwesterners—big, heavy meals. Eat until you have to unbutton your pants, take a nap in front of the TV, and go to bed. I guess there wasn't much else to look forward to—after a long hard day's work—besides my mother's amazing home cooking. But this is the reason that my parents weigh 600 pounds between them (they both have diabetes) and I have to wonder every day if I'm going to get a phone call that my father's had a heart attack.

While the Midwest is the fattest region in the country, we can all relate to having learned bad habits as a child. When I was a kid, I didn't know those meals were fattening and caused heart disease. I was a little kid, she was my mom, and moms know best. Whatever part of the world you grew up in, there's some kind of amazing food that should only be eaten in moderation. In the South, you have BBQ spare ribs and cornbread. In the East, you have pasta and pizza. And in the West, you've got spicy Mexican food covered in cheese. The problem is, we eat these foods all too often, and we eat way too much of them.

And, of course, I can't blame everything on my mom. She was always trying to get me to eat vegetables (canned or otherwise), which I hated, just like every other kid in the world.

Sometimes she would steam carrots for dinner, and we weren't allowed to leave the table until all of our carrots were gone. Eventually, I discovered a way to force the carrots down my throat—there was always a giant bottle of ketchup on the table, no matter what meal we were having. I got the ingenious idea to cover my carrots in ketchup, so I could leave the table and go play with my G.I. Joes. (Why in the hell kids hate vegetables, I'll never understand. Shit, it took me twenty-eight years to learn to like them! I guess it's because they don't taste as good as, say, ice cream. But I think that's all relative. Once you realize how good something is for you and how sexy it will make you look, it starts to taste better. When you're a little kid, however, you don't care about looking sexy—you care about Kool-Aid and pudding pops.)

When I became a grown-up, moved away from the nest, and had to learn to feed myself, my diet plan became similar to the way I'd been raised—I had eight to ten meals that I rotated: chicken Pad Thai, sesame chicken, grilled chicken club sandwiches, turkey sandwiches, Borrachos, tacos, Reubens, and burgers. Seriously, that's all I ate from the ages of twenty to twenty-eight. Every day when I woke up at two P.M., I thought about what I wanted to eat, and those were my options. (When you wake up with a hangover, the last thing on your mind is a salad, and the first thing is pork-fried rice.) Occasionally, I had a couple extra bucks to go out to dinner with my buddies, and I'd watch them all order really strange things that I'd never heard of, like calamari. After growing up in Nebraska, I thought eating Pad Thai was a fucking *cultural* experience. I just had no idea that it had 2,000mg of sodium, or that it was making me fat and bloated.

STEP 1: NO MORE EATING AT NIGHT

My quest to get sexy started the same day that I came back to NYC after visiting my parents for a week during Christmas vacation. No, it wasn't some New Year's resolution bullshit. I don't believe in that crap. The way I figure, if you want to change something in your life, just fucking change it! You don't need an excuse or a reason. Nobody sticks to their New Year's resolutions anyway. It just happened that that's when I finally found all the motivation I needed, and it was the perfect time to stop eating like shit—I still had a few months to wear my winter clothes and leather jackets. If it had been June and I was already wearing T-shirts, everyone would have been able to see my fat gut bouncing around, and I probably would've just said, *Fuck it. Everyone already knows that I'm fat. It just doesn't matter.* But this particular January I was ready. I knew the sexiest man on the planet was in there somewhere, underneath all those buffalo wings and Budweisers.

Not that I had any kind of a plan in the beginning. I had no idea what a "healthy" meal looked like, or how often I should be working out (or even what to do when and if I ever did get my ass to the gym). I decided that it's best to start with small, subtle changes. If you try to do too much, too fast—like going from eating only fried, fatty foods one day to eating only tofu the next—you're just setting yourself up for failure. I mean, there's a reason they tell drug addicts to wean themselves off the smack slow and steady—withdrawal is a bitch. I *did* know that eating at night—or in my case, at four in the morning—was bad because your metabolism slows down while you're sleeping. Actually, everything slows down while you're sleeping, so your body can rest and recharge for the next day. It's Diet 101. I knew I had to start somewhere, so when I got back to New York, the first thing I said to myself was, "That's it! No more eating at night!" Cutting out that late-night meal was the first step I took to sexy.

I go to bed at five or six in the morning on nights that I'm working at the bar. Since my shifts start at nine or ten P.M., I decided that would be my cutoff time. From the second I stepped behind that bar to start my shift, that was it—no more food until morning. If you have a regular nine-to-five job, and you go to bed after Letterman every night, there's no reason you should be eating anything after seven or eight P.M.

This was extremely difficult for me, at first. I'd still go to the deli with my buddies after work, to get scratch-off tickets and drink a few more beers, and I'd watch them all get Borrachos (even though it's my fucking sandwich). Instead, I'd order turkey on whole wheat, with cheese, mayo, and tomatoes (never lettuce). I'd throw it in the fridge when I got home and dream about it all night. Then I'd wake up and eat the shit out of it; I'd stand there in the kitchen, in my underwear, and devour that sandwich like I was a python in the Amazon. It tasted so much better knowing that I hadn't eaten a huge meat sandwich right before bed. Plus, not feeling like a fat, bloated bastard first thing in the morning meant that I was actually starting to accomplish things during the day, like cleaning my room and going to the gym (more on that later). Looking back on it now, it seems like such an easy, simple change, but at the time it was hard as hell.

The real problem here, when you're dieting but you're still drinking, is the "Drunk Munchies." For ten years, I had come home wasted and ordered a pizza or called the diner for a delivery. Then I'd pass out with a pastrami Reuben just sitting there in my colon, rotting away into a fat mess that wouldn't want to get out of bed in the morning. I had to force myself to go to bed without eating. Even if I ate a light snack, it was trouble. If I'm wasted, my self-control is gone. Actually, self-control is a problem for me drunk or sober. But when you're drunk, your body encourages you to eat as much as possible to soak up all that booze. Plus, everyone loves a good midnight snack (or an extra-large pizza).

Once in a while, when I was *really* drunk, I'd put the sandwich in the fridge after work and I wouldn't be able to help myself—I'd be back ten minutes later, shoving it down my gullet as fast as possible. But I only allowed this to happen a few times, and I'd beat myself up all day the next day, mad at not having enough self-control to stay away from food at four in the morning.

Pretty quickly, I realized that cutting out that extra meal right before bed was working. I started to drop a few pounds. I couldn't believe it! I had lost weight, and all I had to do was cut out that fourth meal of the day. For the other three meals, I just stuck with the unhealthy crap I'd been eating for years. For the first week or so, that was enough.

TAKING IT ONE DAY AT A TIME

For the first month of my "diet," I kept drinking beer. Hell, I didn't even switch to light beer. Budweiser has 5 percent alcohol, 145 calories, and 10.6g of carbs. Bud Light has 4.2 percent alcohol, 110 calories, and 6.6g of carbs. If there were a drunkness-to-calorie ratio, Bud and Bud Light would be pretty equal. If you want to get drunk, stick with the "Red and White Dynamite," because it tastes like real beer.

I also kept smoking cigarettes. Yeah, that's right. I said it. I'm not a doctor; I'm a real fucking person. So what if smoking kills you? So does getting hit by a bus. And when I tell you I was a smoker, I'm not fucking around. I smoked two packs a day. I smoked in my house, I smoked in my bed; if I woke up in the middle of the night (or really, really early in the morning), I'd suck down Camel Lights while I was pissing. I couldn't even make it up the stairs without losing my breath, and I blamed it on the cigarettes. Eventually, after all this effort to lose weight and get in shape, I became totally addicted to running. (It sounds crazy, I know. But very soon, you'll get high on running, too— or basketball, or surfing, whatever gets your ass off the couch.) The more addicted to running I became, the more I started thinking about quitting smoking. But for those first months, I just enjoyed it too damn much. *Fuck that*, I said. *I'll quit when I'm good and goddamn ready.*

Back to my diet. I wasn't about to give up all the foods I loved all at once, so I kept going to my favorite diner, but I'd try order-ing a side of vegetables with my burger instead of French fries. (I knew that having the fries in front of me would be way too tempting to resist, so I avoided that completely and told every-one to hold my fries.) French fries, by the way, are like that smoking-hot girl who's just a little too beautiful for her own good. You know she's bad for you. You know she's crazy, and she's going to do things to you that you are not going to like. Your friends are going to hate her, yet she's impossible to resist. Here's the thing, you'd be much better off going with the somewhat good-looking girl, the one with a good head on her shoulders and no daddy issues. This girl has a real job, which means she's not a model or an actress. The model is bad for you, the good girl will make your life better. For lack of a better term, let's call this type of girl—the good girl—a vegetable.*

---

*Vegetable (vej-tə-bəl): N. Female.
  1. A somewhat good-looking girl with a good head on her shoulders and no daddy issues, with a real job. Not a model or an actress.
  2. An attractive girl who reads a lot of books and has at least one cat.
She's pretty hot, but she's a vegetable; she just wants to watch Friends *and cuddle all night.*

When I first started my "diet," my buddies would bust my balls for ordering healthy food. *Oh, he's on a* diet, *what a pussy.* I hated it, but I also knew they were just making fun of something that they knew nothing about, something they wished they had the balls to do, too. It's not much different than when one of the guys grows a mustache or changes his haircut. Guys aren't always comfortable with change. Soon enough, the ball-busting turned to praise: "Damn, bro, you're looking good! Have you been working out?"

Yes, dumbass. Remember when you made fun of me for ordering broccoli? Who's got the better chance of scoring the hot chick now? I was already feeling so much better about the way I looked, actually, that I stopped thinking of vegetables as "asparagus" or "string beans"; I was thinking of them as "confidence" and "sex." (Try ordering a side of steamed sex with your burger.)

I quickly developed an interest in fruit, too. Tony, the guy I work with on Friday nights, always gets a bag of chips and a banana to munch on sometime during the night. So one night when I was at the deli, I got myself a banana, too (no chips for me; even this idiot knew that chips were bad for you). The banana . . . wow, what a genius invention! It's a perfect food. I hadn't eaten much fruit in my life until that night; it just never really crossed my mind. I didn't know how to pick out produce at the grocery store. I didn't even know what some of the weird-looking fruit was. I mean, fuck. My mother fed me canned peaches. How was I supposed to pick out a real peach? In fact, the first few times that I actually went to the grocery store, I'd walk right past all the fresh fruit, straight to the milk section in the back. Then I'd cruise over to the frozen dinner section for some Lean Cuisines. I didn't know that if you ate two or three of them at once, they'd make you fat. The package says "lean" for fuck's sake. Anyway, those Friday night bananas eventually turned into an obsession for fruit.

THE BIRTH OF A CHEAT DAY

During my transformation, I decided that once a week I would allow myself to eat whatever I wanted, guilt-free. Since I throw a BBQ nearly every Sunday—with potato salad, cheddarwurst, turkey sausage, brats, beer, and Lynyrd Skynyrd on the radio— Sundays seemed like an excellent day for a "Cheat Day."

Sunday night is also bowling night. I love bowling. One day, I hope to be on one of those Sunday afternoon bowling shows on TV, wearing tight spandex pants with no shirt on, kicking all those old fucks' asses. Anyway, every Sunday night my buddy, Mexico, and I would drink some beers and then go bowling. I call him Mexico because, you know, that's where he's from, and we worked together at the taco shop. He's got a lazy eye and he seems to idolize me a little bit. He even grew his hair long like mine. I don't mind the adoration; he's a nice kid—until he gets wasted. I've had to break up many fights because he got completely shit-drunk and grabbed some chick's ass. I've even thrown him out of my bar on several occasions. But he always calls me the next day and apologizes. "I'm really sorry, man. I'm so stupid." Where do I find all these completely inappropriate friends?

After the bowling alley threw us out every Sunday, Mexico and I would pick up a few six-packs and go back to my place to watch cowboy movies, get drunk, and order pizza and chicken wings. (By the time I got home from bowling, I'd worked up another appetite. And after eating relatively healthy foods for six straight days, pizza is amazing. I could eat the whole damn pie in three minutes and pass out.) You see, for those first few weeks, I'd be so fucked up from a day of drinking that I'd forget about my late-night eating rule. The outcome was that I'd wake up on Monday morning weighing six pounds more than I had when I woke up on Sunday morning. I also had a hell of a time putting on my running shoes.

So on my Sunday "Eat Anything Day," I started reminding myself: If you want to stay fat, go ahead and eat the last burger that's been sitting on the picnic table for three hours, and finish off the potato salad while watching *SpongeBob*, waiting for your one A.M. pizza delivery. But if you want to be sexy, you must resist the Beer Munchies. Fight them off like Rocky vs. the Russian. Just drink a bunch of cold water and go to bed. You will thank yourself in the morning.

THE FIRST PLATEAU

January went by faster than I could have imagined. I stayed positive, took everything one day at a time, and didn't trick myself into thinking that if I didn't drop twenty pounds in one month that I was a loser and might as well give up. And when that first month was over, I stepped on the scale and discovered that I'd already dropped ten pounds! I still didn't look like one of those airbrushed magazine guys, but I was excited.

Very soon after that, however, I reached my first plateau. I got so frustrated that I was ready to give up and start eating cheeseburgers three times a day. I was doing all the same things I'd been doing during that first month. Unfortunately, the first ten pounds are the easiest to lose. My body was on to me now; it knew what I was up to, and it had switched into survival mode.

What the fuck is a *Plateau?*
Plateau: A level or period of
stability; a leveling off

No, we're not talking about scaling a flat fucking mountain somewhere in the Southwest. A "plateau" occurs when you've been losing weight and seeing results, and then all of a sudden you get stuck; you hover around the same weight—for a period of several weeks or more—and can't figure out why. Basically, it's when you've been making some progress toward becoming the sexiest man on the planet, and then you reach a point where your sexy stops increasing.

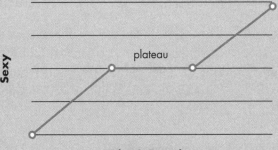

Diet & Exercise

The main reason everyone eventually experiences this incredibly frustrating situation is because the amount of calories you burn is largely related to your overall body mass. For example, if you're a dude who weighs 300 pounds, it's gonna take more effort—and therefore more calories—to get your fat ass off the sofa than if you were a tiny guy who only weighed a buck fifty. Once you lose some weight, however, your metabolism adjusts— you won't burn as many calories just by breathing, blinking, and farting as you did when your ass was the size of Cleveland. When you reach a plateau, you know it's probably time to switch up your diet and workout routine.

The human body was not designed to look the way modern humans want it to look. Remember our little history lesson on ancient man? If you were a caveman roaming the earth for food three thousand years ago, you'd kill a buffalo and eat as much as possible. It might be days before you found anything else to eat, so your body stores this food as fat, in case you run out of arrows. That's why I wasn't losing as much weight as I had in the previous weeks. Even though I was eating the same healthier diet, my body had adjusted and was learning new ways to store fat. I had to learn how to outsmart it. You've got to be very careful when you reach a plateau. It's too easy to just say, *Fuck it. I've lost as much as I'm going to lose*, and then go back to eating shit. This is a good way to wind up heavier than when you started.

Still, I spent that entire second month pissed off. I was down and out. I'd gone nearly three weeks without losing a single pound. But I stuck with it. I kept eating vegetables, and kept forcing myself to stay away from French fries, fried chicken, and all those other fatty foods that would have comforted me through such a disappointing time. It's incredibly frustrating to work at something and not get any results. Day after day, I was forcing myself to do things that I didn't really want to do, like eat vegetables and get my ass to the gym. But no matter how much I didn't want to do something, I knew that what I really didn't want was to be fat anymore. I kept putting on my running shoes and hitting the pavement. Before long I broke through, and lost a few more pounds.

Looking back now on those first few months, it's amazing the difference that just a few pounds makes. My smile was brighter, my jokes were funnier—I was really beginning to feel like a better person. Not only was I fixing something that had bothered me for most of my life (my weight), I was accomplishing goals. I was doing things that, in the past, I had only *wished* I had the balls to do, like trying new foods or signing up for a spin class. (Yes, I actually took a spin class. I'll tell you about it later.) There's a big difference between losing a few pounds and getting the dream body you've always wanted, but it was losing those first few pounds that gave me the motivation I needed to keep pushing. I was starting to see what happens when you earn something you really want.

I used to wear T-shirts with a pocket on the chest to help cover up at least one of my man boobs. Then one day, after I had lost about fifteen pounds (about two and a half to three months into my diet), I decided to go out and buy a thin T-shirt with no pocket—a medium, one size smaller than usual, just for the hell of it. I remember how nervous I was in the store. I kept thinking to myself, *Stay positive, fucker. If you get home and look like shit in this shirt, that does not mean you're going to give up and go back to being a fat ass!* When I got home and tried it on, it was still way too tight. But did I give up and start eating hot dogs again? No. It inspired me to push even harder. I was going to get myself into that shirt if it fucking killed me. And just a few short weeks later, I had to go out and buy more of those shirts because it was all I was wearing. A few weeks after that, I had to buy the same shirt again—in a *small*.

The same thing happened with jeans. I wear girls' jeans. I have for years. I don't even know what size I am in men's jeans. And for years, I had one pair that fit like a glove, size 11 Long; I'd wear them for three weeks without washing them. Then I got up the balls to buy myself the same pair one size smaller, so I could try them on at home and see how they fit. Now I'm all the way down to a 5 Long and loving every skinny minute of it. (For anyone who thinks a size 5 is pretty small, remember, God didn't give me hips—girl's jeans just fit differently.)

I'll never forget the day I finally got rid of my fat jeans—I even took a picture of them first, to memorialize the experience. I had worked my ass off (literally), and I wasn't about to undo all that by shoving hamburgers down my throat.

CHAPTER THREE

Your Body Is a Hot Rod

LÜC'S LAW: I AM SMARTER THAN MY FOOD.

I have the attention span of a three-year-old, and I've never been much of a reader. As a matter of fact, about the only book I remembered finishing—before my quest to get sexy, that is—was *The Dirt: Confessions of the World's Most Dangerous Rock Band*, by Mötley Crüe. But the more I got into working out and looking good, the more I wanted to read about health and fitness. I wanted to know what was happening to my body, what certain foods did for me that others couldn't.

The way I see it, if a man wants to become a doctor or a lawyer, or anything worth doing, he goes to school. Well, I didn't have the time or the money for school (and it hadn't worked out so well the first time), so I had to figure things out on my own. I needed a plan. I subscribed to a bunch of fitness magazines. I started going to the cereal aisle at the supermarket and reading the sides of all the boxes. And I started searching the Internet for things like "MSG," "protein," and "reps per set." I also went to the health and fitness sections at the bookstore, and read diet book after diet book (and hated every minute of it).

Here's the God's honest truth: I've learned three things from all the time, money and effort I spent reading books and articles and magazines and nutrition labels.

1. Anything labeled "diet" is terrible for you.
2. The FDA is full of shit.
3. The "experts" are no help at all.

For example, a bunch of doctors and other assholes recommend that the healthy amount of weight to lose—per week—is one to two pounds. Since there are 3,500 calories per pound of body fat, that means that cutting out 1,000 calories a day, for seven days a week, translates to a two-pound weight loss. (Seven thousand calories total, dumbass.) Coincidentally, if your caloric intake were to remain constant (meaning you eat the same shit you normally do), and you were to burn off 1,000 calories per day, that would also translate to two pounds per week gone. In other words, to lose a healthy amount of weight per week, you've got to cut out 1,000 calories a day, burn off 1,000 calories a day, or figure out some combination of the two.

So there you have it, the scientific fucking formula for losing weight. Unfortunately, it's not quite as simple as following this formula. It can take years before you fully understand the perfect amount of calories you should be taking in on a daily basis. And who's to say there should be one set number? Maybe on Monday your magic number of calories is 2,200, and on Tuesday it's 1,800. (And who the fuck wants to actually count calories anyway?) The truth is that everybody's body is different, and what works for me may not always work for you. I like blondes, you like redheads. Other than that, diet books are really a whole bunch of crap written by a whole bunch of assholes who think they know more about your body than you do.

You know what else is bullshit? Those airbrushed women with six-pack abs—they're on the cover of every one of those diet books. If you ask me, they are the reason that there's so much obesity in America. Let's say a regular everyday guy, like a plumber, finally gets enough balls to go into a bookstore and ask where the weight-loss section is. (That step alone is more than most men are willing to take.) Then he gets to this section, and every book has a girl in a sports bra with seventeen abs on the cover. This girl would *never* go on a date with him anyway, so why the fuck would she care whether or not he's fat? He's not even going to pick that book up, because he's intimidated by this over-chiseled example of the human body. I know this because I was that guy. I may have had enough balls to go to the weight-loss section of my local bookstore, but I never found a book that seemed like it would work for someone like me.

And what about women? Women are much more interested in dieting than men. (Why? Because it's not a *faux pas* for women to diet in the first place.) But why would a woman who is unhappy with her body want to learn how to change her life from some fitness model who's been into working out since the day she was born? What does the girl with seventeen abs know about being overweight and insecure and miserable? She's shredded and beautiful, and probably always has been.

After reading all this horseshit, I knew I was going to have to take matters into my own hands. After all, I am a man, a human being. I'm at the top of the food chain. I am the smartest and most advanced of all the species. I am certainly smarter than the cow on my plate. I am better than the chocolate pastries at the bakery. Cheeseburgers and birthday cake would not exist without the intelligence of man. Therefore, I should be smart enough to figure out what to eat and when to eat it.

PREMIUM UNLEADED

I am a car freak. I love American muscle cars, and I used to own two hot rods, Ginger and Nadine. (I no longer own Nadine, but Ginger is alive and well.) I *understand* cars, and I've been tinkering under the hood for years. That's why I started to think of my body as a machine. It helped to compare my body to the engine of a car, because that's what made sense to me—it was just easier to relate to my body as a machine than an actual living organism. Cars and humans are very similar in nature, actually. My heart is my fuel pump, my lungs are my carburetors, adrenaline

GINGER.

is my pistons, my legs are the gear box, my eyes are the headlights, my stomach is the gas tank, and my colon is my exhaust pipe. Most important, my mouth is where I put the fuel. (I only hope my body lasts as long as my car has.)

Automobiles, of course, have one huge advantage over human beings—they don't have emotions. Cars can eat the same thing every day and still run perfectly. People, unfortunately, have taste buds and cravings. Every time we eat an ice cream sandwich, for example, a chemical in our brain yells out, "I like this. Give me more of this. Ice cream makes me happy."

These days, ice cream no longer sends a signal to my brain that says "this makes me happy"; it sends a signal to my brain that says, "you're a fat ass." This guy would rather be a high-performance hot rod doing nine-second quarter-miles than spending my hard-earned money at Ben & Jerry's.

Once I understood that the performance of my machine (my body) depended on the quality of the gas I put in (the food), I was able to start making smarter decisions about what to eat. My "diet" wasn't going to be about limiting myself to a certain number of calories per day, or choosing foods based on some kind of points system, or eating a certain percentage of fats and a certain percentage of carbs, or getting into "the zone." I just wanted to eat quality foods that weren't processed all to hell. My body used to run on diesel fuel, and by slowly weeding out all the crap, I was switching to premium unleaded.

For example, I've always had a tremendous love for ketchup and all things associated with it. But I went straight to my fridge and threw that shit away. Anything involving ketchup is bad—burgers, fries, onion rings—and any idiot knows that shit will not help you lose weight. I didn't know what I was going to eat if I could never have a cheeseburger again, but I knew I was ready for a change.

I also went through my cupboards and threw away everything I thought might be fattening, and anything with any ingredients that I couldn't pronounce. Actually, I threw away pretty much everything that was in there. This didn't take long. I was a single guy, my kitchen was empty most of the time, and most of my meals were delivered to my door by a little guy on a bike who didn't speak English.

I also threw away the milk. I've never been a huge fan of

milk, and I started really thinking about where it comes from. Milk is made by nature to turn baby cows into big cows. *If you want to be a big cow,* I thought to myself, *keep drinking milk.*

What I found out is that pasteurization, without all the scientific terms, is basically the act of processing milk with chemicals so it's "safe" for humans to drink. But if you've ever been to a dairy farm, it's not a pretty sight. The cows' udders are often infected because they're hooked up to metal machines all day that rarely get cleaned. In fact, dairy products manufactured in America are filled with all kinds of crap that would make you throw up. I knew I needed calcium because that's what bones are made of and I didn't want my bones being eaten away by my own body, so I picked up some calcium supplements. I also researched foods other than dairy products that are high in calcium, like broccoli and almonds, and slowly started mixing them into my diet. (Eventually, I gave up the supplements. Plenty of foods have calcium in them. Why cheat with a fucking pill?)

What the fuck is Salt?
Salt: A mineral (sodium chloride), used as a food seasoning and preservative

When I got serious about reading the nutritional labels, I decided I wouldn't buy foods with ingredients I couldn't pronounce. In fact, I started buying everything fresh. I quit eating things that came out of package or a box, and I cut out things completely that listed salt in the ingredients.

At first I thought salt was okay. I mean, sodium is crucial to the body; it regulates nerve impulses and muscle contractions, and works with potassium to control the movement of water in and out of the cells. And most foods have enough *natural* salt in them to keep your body healthy. But in the old days, manufacturers added loads of salt to foods to save themselves some money, because the salt allows a product to sit on the shelf longer, rather than decomposing and having to be thrown out. Things are different since the invention of preservatives, but salt still runs rampant—it covers up the lack of flavor in packaged foods.

If you're the type of person who actually uses the saltshaker at the dinner table, you're in big trouble, because even though salt won't necessarily make you gain weight, it does tend to make you hungrier. (Plenty of studies have shown that salt makes you thirsty, and hunger and thirst are closely related.) Nothing in your diet is as variable as sodium chloride (salt). If you're a lazy fuck, your body doesn't need much to survive. If you work out a lot, it's possible to sweat out 2,000mg of sodium in an hour. Any time you sweat, you lose salt from your body. This means that your true Recommended Daily Allowance (RDA) of sodium—randomly set by experts at 2,500mg a day—is actually somewhere between 500mg a day (when you sit in front of your TV with the air-conditioning on for sixteen straight hours), and something like 12,000mg (on the day you run a half-marathon).

Too much sodium can lead to hypertension, edema, and even osteoporosis. But don't blame salt. Blame our society's lousy eating habits. The average American diet consists of twice the RDA of salt. It's no goddamn wonder heart disease is such a big deal in this country! Many of your favorite foods are available with **No Salt Added**. And if they're not, it's time to find some new favorite foods. Put the salt down!

Now that I had thrown away most of the crap in my kitchen, it was time to start replacing that crap with quality food. The first *really* healthy meal I ate was from an organic pita place in my neighborhood that I had stumbled across on the Internet. I've never actually been to this place, but I've had those fuckers on speed dial for years now. I must have called them every day for a month. I started out ordering the chicken platter, which came with a bunch of lettuce that I didn't eat. I picked around it, eating the chicken and the rice, and sometimes a vegetable or two. Then I discovered a dish they made with grilled chicken, brown rice, sun-dried tomatoes, raisins, and bits of feta cheese. It was delicious and it was big; the meal filled me up and I felt satisfied. I'd heard that brown rice was good for you. Back then, I didn't know why or what the difference was between brown rice and white rice, but I liked it. I ordered this dish every day for two months. I actually worried that the people taking the phone orders would get sick of me calling. I also lived kind of far away from the place, so I made sure to tip the delivery guys like crazy so they'd keep coming back. I had finally found something to eat that I enjoyed, and that wasn't terrible for me. I felt amazing.

I lost a few more pounds, and kept searching for healthy things to eat. That's when I discovered the California wrap from the diner. It came with a small salad, for which I would substitute a side of steamed vegetables or broccoli to nibble on to help fill me up. Even if I only ate two or three pieces of broccoli, I felt like it was a success. Sometimes I actually ate all of it, and the next day I would take a decent shit for a change. There is nothing worse than being bloated and constipated, and I had been bloated and constipated for twenty-eight years. Hell, I would've done anything for a decent shit, and the vegetables helped.

Looking back on it now, I can't believe the crap that I used to eat. I had no idea how bad it was for my body. My brown rice bowl and California wraps were teaching me that there might be even more foods out there that I could enjoy, or at least tolerate; foods that would make me healthier and sexier.

For example, there's a fish restaurant right next to my bar, so I started ordering a grilled fish dish with some vegetables and shrimp on the side for dinner before work. I had no idea that this was what a healthy meal actually looked like. In fact, I'd never eaten a filet of fish until that restaurant opened (and I only ordered it because they gave me a discount). My brother and I used to go fishing with my dad and grandfather all the time when I was a kid. Mom and Grandma would fry it up for dinner, but I never ate it. Why didn't I eat it, you ask? Because my dad didn't eat it. Why didn't my dad eat it? Probably because his dad didn't eat it, either. Real men in the Midwest don't eat anything other than steak and hamburger . . . and maybe pizza, from time to time. Men eat meat. Women eat fish; it's a chick food. In fact, my mother would often grill herself some salmon while the boys were eating burgers. She'd always ask if we wanted to try it, but we'd always say no. I guess fish is just weird to kids. (Though why fish would be any weirder than a cow, I'll never understand.) Frozen fish sticks were the closest thing I'd ever eaten to real fish, and I only ate them when there was nothing else in the house and my mom was busy at work. I'd drench them in ketchup, of course.

These days, I actually buy fresh fish and cook it on my George Foreman grill. I still hate that I have to clean that damn thing, but fresh fish is delicious, and so good for my sexy body that it's worth it. Of course, I still love the occasional steak, but it usually clogs me up and I won't shit for two days. Now I only eat red meat once in a blue moon.

NO MORE FUCKING AROUND

It didn't take long before I gave up eating high-calorie, high-fat foods altogether. My typical dinner turned into two cans of tuna, heated up in the microwave in a paper bowl. I'd mix in some black beans, cover it in mustard, add a little pepper, and that was dinner. No fat, hardly any carbs, lots of protein, and very few calories. If I felt like treating myself, I'd put all that inside a whole-wheat tortilla, turning it into a ghetto wrap. It's not like this is the most exciting meal ever concocted, but the fact that there were no dirty plates or pans to clean up made it taste pretty great. The fact that I was losing weight made it taste like something you'd see on the Food Network. I ate tuna with mustard for a month straight.

Eventually the tuna got boring and, at the same time, I hit another plateau. For whatever reason, what I'd been doing wasn't working anymore. So I started eating more salads. Even though I'd always hated lettuce, I quickly learned that salads are key for weight loss—leafy greens, aside from being *very* low in calories, are packed with vitamins and energy that keep your metabolism running at full speed. (Greens are also a necessity for taking huge, glorious dumps; that was enough to make me a believer.) That doesn't mean, however, that you can shove your face with a Buffalo Chicken Caesar salad. You might as well order a burger with blue cheese if you're going to eat that crap. I'm talking about a nice salad of mixed greens and vegetables, topped with oil and vinegar dressing—no croutons or Ranch dressing. These days, I make myself order salads as often as I possibly can. I've gone an entire week on nothing but salads.

I also added almonds to my work-night snack. I had read that almonds were packed with protein and monosaturated (good) fat but, at first, I didn't understand how that would help. I thought that if you wanted to lose weight, you had to cut out all fats completely. That's because somewhere along the way, fat became a dirty word. As Americans, we are fucking terrified of the word "fat." Yet loads of people will stuff their faces with all sorts of plastic man-made crap simply because the package says "Fat: 0g." This is horseshit.

The fact is, unless you're dealing with a piece of fruit, what you should be afraid of is anything that has *zero* grams of fat. How did they make it taste so good without fat? A lot of research and bullshit, that's how. You've been brainwashed to think that anything containing 2g of fat will make you look four months pregnant. If you could take all those minutes you spent in the grocery store obsessing over labels and buying pre-packaged foods that say "low-fat" or "no-fat," and spend those minutes lifting a twenty-pound dumbbell, you wouldn't have to worry about what it says on the side of the damn package.

Still not convinced? One day I went to see my hairdresser—who's the lead stylist of a hit show on Broadway—and she noticed that I had some almonds with me. I explained that almonds were my new thing. Then she told me that one of the dancers in her show, a guy with the best body she'd ever seen, eats almonds constantly. I thought to myself, *Wow. Here I am carrying around almonds, just like a guy with the best body this chick's ever seen. I must be doing something right.*

There are, of course, good fats and bad fats, however. Potato chips, for example, are bad fat. But if you eat the right amount of good fats, your body will be an Italian sports car. Flaxseed oil, for example, is a great source of good fat. Olive oil, almonds, and avocados are also good. My favorite guilty pleasure is peanut butter. (I say guilty only because more often than not, I can't resist going back for more.) Just be sure to buy one that says "Ingredients: peanuts." There shouldn't be anything else in there. I eat a couple of tablespoons with an apple for dessert.

Peanut butter, like many other products that come in a package (including margarine, mayonnaise, and ketchup), by the way, has changed over the years based on the public's perception of what is or is not "healthy." For example, some-time in the early 1990s the low-fat craze went into full effect. Right around the same time, food manufacturers had to start listing ingredients and nutritional information on the sides of all their pretty packages. All of a sudden, people realized that peanut butter has about 20g of fat per serving and started freaking the fuck out. Sales dropped, and the assholes that make fake peanut butter sprung into action. "If the people want low fat, we better figure out a way to give it to them!"

How do you remove fat from a peanut? It's not possible. So what did they do? They added more high-fructose corn syrup and less peanuts. The general public is so stupid, they fell for it! The label says it has a fewer grams of fat, it must be better for me!

Pull your heads out of your asses, people. Fat is one of the most important elements in a healthy diet. Without it, your body can't function. Your hair will start falling out and your skin will look like shit. Put down the Clearasil and eat a table-spoon of all-natural peanut butter.

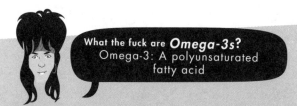

What the fuck are Omega-3s?
Omega-3: A polyunsaturated fatty acid

People see Omega-3 on a carton of eggs and they're willing to pay an extra three dollars for the dozen. Fucking marketing. People assume they *need* these Omega-3s. The thing is, you're already getting them.

Omega-3 fatty acids are fats found naturally in lots of foods: nuts, oils (like olive oil), cold water fish like salmon and tuna, and soybeans. The Omega-3 *fad*, however, was brought on by the tofu fad. Tofu manufacturers got together and said, "We need a reason for people to eat more tofu." So they made Omega-3s popular. Even though any human eating a halfway decent diet is already getting enough Omega-3s, all of a sudden, people thought they had to have more—or they would die. We think Omega-3s are some miracle drug that can cure cancer and heal joints.

My point is, don't buy into the Omega-3 hype. Yes, foods that naturally contain Omega-3 fatty acids are good for you; you might even want to eat more of them. But foods that are *fortified* with Omega-3s aren't going to do you much good. If you buy eggs or tortilla chips with "added" Omega-3s, for example, all that means is that Omega-3s weren't in those foods naturally. Manufacturers basically just injected these foods, and eating them isn't nearly as effective as eating a little bit of fish once or twice a week. If you really want to increase the amount of Omega-3s in your diet, buy some flax-seed oil at the health food store and put half a tablespoon in your shake in the morning. Don't spend the extra three dollars on the eggs. This is bullshit.

FUCK YOU, DIET SODA. AND FUCK YOU, TOO, CHEESE.

At this point—by some fucking miracle, and a combination of a lot of running, hitting the gym, and completely changing my diet—I had lost about twenty-five pounds. I still had some flab on the back of my arms, in my gut, and in my bitch tits, but I was getting pretty close—much closer, in fact—to the body I'd always wanted; close enough to *taste* it. I was willing to do whatever it took to trim off those last few pounds of fat. So I did a little bit more research, and I decided that there were only three things left in my diet that were keeping me from becoming a high-performance machine: cheese, caffeine, and booze. I sure as hell wasn't going to cut out booze, so let's start with cheese.

I used to eat cheese with everything—turkey clubs, sub sandwiches, salads; it was even in my chicken and brown rice bowls. But several months into my diet, I decided to give up cheese, just to see what would happen. Within days I noticed I was shitting more regularly. I wasn't bloated or constipated as often as I used to be. That was all it took for me. From that day on, I never touched another piece of cheese again. (I already told you, I'd tossed the milk a while ago.) I hate the fact that this puts me one step closer to becoming a pretentious Smiths fan–type of shit head, but kiss my ass, world. I don't eat cheese and I'm sexier than you.

On the very same day that I decided to say good-bye to cheese, I decided to kick caffeine's ass, too. This, I worried, probably wouldn't be so easy. Every Monday for the past three years, I had bought myself a Subway sandwich, a bag of chips, and a root beer for lunch. I looked forward to that root beer all week. Every other day, I drank Diet Dr Pepper—it was like my coffee. I've never been a coffee drinker, but I still needed my fake-sugar/caffeine rush. At the time, I didn't know that diet sodas had something in them called aspartame, an artificial sweetener that gives people cancer and diabetes. I just knew they had zero calories, so I thought I was being smart.

I'd read somewhere that caffeine is bad for your digestive system, and I had been drinking diet soda like a crack head. I knew I was addicted, and I didn't want to be addicted to anything anymore—other than cigarettes, of course. At first, I was only planning on cutting out diet soda for a few days, just to see what would happen. And to be honest, I didn't really think it would make a difference. I just wanted to prove to myself that I could quit, and then I figured I'd go back to drinking diet soda, since I was addicted. A day or two after giving it up, I noticed I wasn't crashing an hour after every meal, like I usually did. I had no idea that caffeine had been controlling my life like that! I just assumed that mid-afternoon crash was how my body worked. Around five P.M., when I used to get tired and need a nap—or another diet soda—I was suddenly feeling great, and ready to tackle whatever it was that needed doing. Ever since the day I gave up caffeine, the only liquid I've put in my mouth is a shit-load of water and alcoholic beverages.

I suppose all this makes sense; after all, caffeine is a stimulant, a drug. It increases your heart rate, causing your blood vessels to dilate, delivering more oxygen to your brain—that's why you feel a sudden burst of energy when you drink, say, coffee. The effects are only temporary, however; once they wear off, you pour yourself another cup or crack open a diet soda, and now you've got yourself a habit. If you suddenly stop ingesting caffeine, you'll go into withdrawal. Symptoms include headache, nausea, anxiety, and irritability. No fucking thank you.

This was a big day for me. Actually, this might have been *the* day—the day I took down two of my fiercest opponents. For the past ten years, I'd been getting my ass kicked every day by an aluminum can filled with all kinds of man-made crap. I thought diet soda was my friend, but I finally realized that we had a shitty codependent relationship. Diet soda was making me a drug addict, all the while turning my body into a squishy, fluffy mess and preventing me from taking a decent shit. Fuck you, diet soda. And fuck the guy who invented the word "diet," and all of the bullshit products the term is associated with. I'm doing better without you. I kicked your ass right out of my life—and I've got more money in pocket because of it.

What the fuck is *aspartame*?
Aspartame: A man-made sweetener
with almost no calories

This has got to be the dumbest thing ever approved by the FDA. In 1965, a chemist working to develop an antiulcer drug discovered a chemical substance that was more than 100 times sweeter than sugar, yet had no calories. Aspartame, the mother of all artificial sweeteners, was born.

Before applying for FDA approval, the aspartame company decided to test their new substance out on some monkeys. Of the seven monkeys tested, one died and five others had grand mal seizures. Aspartame has also been found to cause holes in the brains of mice. If stored above eighty-four degrees, it turns into liquid formaldehyde.

The FDA was not the least bit interested in approving aspartame, so the company decided to fight fire with fire. (They'd already spent millions developing and testing their new chemical, and they needed FDA approval so they could make their money back.) In 1977, the company hired a Washington insider as the new CEO. This guy brought in a bunch of his cronies as management, which was easy since the aspartame company was willing to pay them all higher wages than they were getting in Washington, anyway. That same year, the aspartame company was involved in a grand jury investigation, for possibly lying about their scientific research and the safety of their sweetener. That's when the aspartame company's law firm decided it would be a great idea to offer the U.S. Attorney—the guy in charge of the investigation—a job. Less than a year later, the U.S. Attorney withdrew from the case and started working for the enemy.

Aspartame was approved for use in dry goods in 1981. In 1983 the first carbonated beverages containing aspartame hit the stores. Guess what else happened? From 1987 to 2009, cases of diabetes in the U.S. rose from 6.5 million to 23.7 million. I'm not saying aspartame is the only reason people get

diabetes, but it's certainly not helping. And have you ever noticed that every time there's a commercial break on TV, there's
also an advertisement for a diabetes testing kit? Diabetes
treatments generate profits of $174 billion annually. Where
do you think all that money goes? If you still want to drink diet
soda after reading that, be my fucking guest.

LEARNING TO LOVE VEGETABLES

Fruits and vegetables, next to protein, became the biggest part
of my diet. The beauty of vegetables is, as long as they aren't
sautéed in butter or prepared in oil, you can eat as much of
them as you damn well please (although, this does not apply to
starchy vegetables, like potatoes and corn on the cob). You can
eat as much cauliflower or spinach as you can stuff in your face
and they'll just make you sexier.

I learned to like the taste of vegetables and my steamer
became my best friend. I'd never had cauliflower in my life
before I bought my steamer. It was weird looking, and I didn't
want anything to do with it. But one day something just clicked
in me, and I started buying lots of different vegetables that I'd
never eaten before. (When I realized that eating vegetables
made my near-constant constipation a thing of the past, that
was really all the motivation I needed.) I'd throw four pieces
of broccoli and four pieces of cauliflower in my steamer with a
couple of chicken breasts. Twenty-five minutes later, lunch was
ready—and I didn't have to do a damn thing except turn on
this machine. I made my own salsa to pour over the chicken,
or I'd pick up a premade version from the health food store—
making sure it only contained things that I was willing to have
running through my bloodstream. So, no crap.

Vegetables are also excellent for snacking, and they're a perfect substitute for potato chips, which just make you a fat, bloated bastard. I'll buy three cucumbers for a dollar, slice them up, and soak them in a bowl of vinegar with some spices—homemade healthy pickles with no salt! (Check out my recipe on page 232.) Or I'll have some baby carrots or grapes.

What the fuck are *Carbs*?
Carbohydrates: Organic compounds that include sugars and starches

This no-carbs craze is a bunch of bullshit. The human body *needs* carbohydrates, which is why they're found in so many types of foods, from rice to bread to sugar to vegetables. Whenever you eat something with carbs, you metabolize those carbs into glucose (sugar), which the body uses as a form of energy. In other words, carbs are fuel. Of course, that doesn't mean that *all* carbs are good for you, or that you can each as much of them as you want.

"Good" carbs—otherwise known as complex carbohydrates—come from raw and unrefined products, like brown rice, fruit, and vegetables. "Bad" carbs, or simple carbohydrates, include white pasta, white bread, and anything with a label that says "enriched." (Simple carbs get broken down quickly by your body, so the energy you get from eating them doesn't last very long; they also cause your blood sugar to spike.) Also, anything with refined (or white) flour is crap and it's bad for you. "Refined" basically means that somebody took out all the nutrients to make it taste better. If you ask me, it doesn't taste better at all.

It is perfectly acceptable to eat carbs while on a diet—just keep your portions down. You shouldn't have more than a tennis ball–sized helping of pasta or rice per day. It's also best to eat all of your carbs early on in the day, and to stay away from carbs after five P.M., since your metabolism slows down while you're sleeping. (Carbs are energy, and you don't need a lot of energy while you're sleeping.) Your body will just store this as fat. In fact, try to eat most of your daily carbs at breakfast. It's always best to eat breakfast right when you wake up; it lets your body and metabolism know that it's time to get to work and start the day.

ROCKET FUEL

About halfway through the third month of my diet, I'd started drinking protein shakes with whey powder after my workouts. Protein is important—it helps you build muscle and burn fat—and this guy at my gym had convinced me I wasn't getting enough. But whey protein mixed with water was getting boring, so I started throwing new and exciting shit into a blender with the protein powder and mixing it up. I call my shakes "Rocket Fuel." Every time I drink one, I feel like I've put on a cape and I'm about to go fly around Metropolis to fight crime.

Rocket Fuel consists of all sorts of ridiculously healthy foods, like a big bag of spinach, arugula, or mixed greens—in fact, anything I pass by in the grocery store that's leafy and green and filled with vitamins, I buy for my shakes. I also buy a couple bags of frozen mixed berries or blueberries. Each bag is 12oz., so I know that needs to make at least three, if not four or five, shakes. Don't cheat and throw a whole bag of berries in there, that's too much sugar and you won't get anywhere. I also might throw in half a banana, or a couple of whole carrots. Then I'll add three scoops of whey, hemp, or rice protein powders, a tablespoon of flaxseed oil for some good healthy fat and, occasionally, if I'm backed up, a big tablespoon of raw psyllium husks. (Psyllium husks are the only important ingredient in those expensive name-brand fiber pills. They put a whole bunch of fillers and other crap in there that you don't need; just go straight to the source.)

I like to get creative with my Rocket Fuel. Sometimes, I'll throw in raw Brussels sprouts, or some broccoli. Anything raw, uncooked, and green is full of vitamins and fiber. I'll throw all that in the blender with some water and mix it up. I feel like Rocky every time I drink one of these fuckers. Or Popeye, with his muscles bulging after eating a can of spinach. I replace a meal with one of these shakes as often as possible. They're around 300–500 calories, so they fill me up and curb my hunger for an hour or two. It's a real meal, it just happens to be one that you drink. (Picture all of those ingredients spread out on a plate, and you can see that it's more than enough for a full meal. It's just not a meal that you'd want to eat like that. Who in the hell wants to eat raw spinach and Brussels sprouts? The truth is, we all should.) The four ounces of berries cut the taste of all the green gross crap (it actually tastes good!). And if you think about how amazing Rocket Fuel is for your body while you're drinking it, it tastes even better. Don't get the wrong impression here. Rocket Fuel isn't exactly a fruit smoothie, but Jamba Juice will make your waistline bulge in no time. Fruit is full of sugar. It's good sugar that your body needs, but you don't need to eat an entire pound of strawberries in one sitting. That's too much sugar for your body to handle at one time.

Two weeks after discovering Rocket Fuel, I had abs. Not bulging magazine abs, but the belly fat had finally started to vanish.

What the fuck is *Whey Protein Powder?*
Whey Protein Powder: A mixture
of proteins isolated from whey, the
liquid created as a by-product of
cheese production

Ever wondered how cheese is made? It starts with milk. In a process called curdling, milk is separated into solid particles called curds (the part that will later be turned into cheese), and whey, a milky-white leftover liquid. You've heard of Little Miss Muffett, eating her curds and whey? Same shit.

Whey *protein* is, obviously, a type of protein that's been isolated from the whey; it's full of amino acids that can help you build muscle and burn fat. This is especially helpful if you want to get shredded, which is why they sell the stuff in big, fat plastic jugs and slap a picture of some huge meathead on the bottle.

DEATH OF A CHEAT DAY

I will remember the Sunday that marked the official end of my cheat days for quite some time. I was at my favorite Mexican restaurant, drinking beers and stuffing my face, watching football. I ate and drank so much that I actually had to go to the bathroom and make myself throw up because my stomach felt like it was going to explode. I was literally in pain from the food I had eaten. I told my friends to order me a shot of tequila and a beer, borrowed a hair tie from the waitress, went to the bathroom, and made myself throw up until my stomach wasn't in pain anymore. I came back from the bathroom, did the shot of tequila, and headed off to the bowling alley.

It's as if the fat guy inside of me had never gone away. He just had to shut the fuck up for six days, then I'd let him make up for being quiet all week by really overdoing it on Sundays. I'd spend the rest of the week trying to get back to the weight I was on the Saturday before I let myself run free at the $4.99 Vegas buffet like some kind of fat ass that may never get another meal. After that Sunday at the Mexican restaurant, I gave up my cheat day indefinitely. I decided it was like a bad girlfriend or worse—Dirty Ice Cream*—that I needed to get rid of to be really happy. If I couldn't control myself on Sunday Funday, then I didn't deserve a fun day at all.

Eventually, I learned to develop a healthier, less compulsive relationship with my food. There's no magical secret to this, by the way, it just takes time and discipline. These days I can indulge a little without losing all self-control and binging on everything and anything I can get my hands on. Occasionally, I'll even let myself go all out with some Thai or Chinese food. At this stage in the game, it's okay to do that. I'd reached my goal weight a long time ago, and I work out so damn often that I know I'll burn off any unwanted calories in a matter of days, anyway.

I still have pizza from time to time, but now I order a small pizza, with no cheese or meat products. (The thought of eating a pizza with no cheese is weird, I know. But give it a shot.) Any meat product you get from a pizza place is going to be heavily processed and full of salt and preservatives. I, of course, can't stop after a couple of slices, which is why I order the small. That way, I don't even have the option of eating the twice-as-big, twice-as-many-calories large. When I've been drinking

---

*Dirty Ice Cream (Dər-tĕ Ĭs-krĕm): N. (Male or Female), V.

    1. A person of the opposite sex with a first impression that's much better than average, but who soon becomes too needy and annoying.

    2. To call or text to the point of annoyance.

    3. A partner that seems sweet in the beginning, but whom you quickly realize is tainted.

She's dirty ice cream. We went on one damn date and she's been blowing me up all fucking week.

for eight straight hours and the guy at the pizza place asks me what size I want, it's incredibly difficult to resist saying "large." It's harder to choose the little pussy small version. (It's also extremely hard to resist saying "... and throw in two orders of buffalo wings and some breadsticks.") That's why I usually ask whoever I'm hanging out with to call and order for me. I wouldn't be ordering food at that time of night in the first place unless I'm drunk and hanging out with someone who also has the munchies.

A small, cheeseless pizza with no meat has around 800–1,000 calories. That may sound like a lot, but it's much better than a cheesy pizza with pepperoni and beef; if you make that a large, your calories end up around 2,500. Order the small and the guilt is cut in half, which makes the pizza twice as enjoyable. Consequently, when I wake up the next day, I don't find myself to be a suicidal, bloated mess.

I no longer think of food as food—it's fuel. In fact, I've completely changed the way I think about eating. When I wake up in the morning, I plan out what I will eat for the entire day. Sometimes I have an entire week's worth of food planned out at once. That way, there's no question that I'll always make the right choices. If I'm recovering from a really rough night, I might allow myself to eat hangover food, but no more than once a week. And by hangover food, I mean getting some hash browns or home fries with an egg-white omelet. After that, and for the next few days, I'll go back to the plan.

CHAPTER FOUR

You Shouldn't Have to Pay Someone to Find Out How Much You Weigh...and Other Reasons Why "Diets" Are Mostly Bullshit

LÜC'S LAW: ALL-YOU-CAN-EAT IS NOT A GOOD THING. I CAN'T BELIEVE I HAVE TO FUCKING EXPLAIN THIS SHIT.

Not too long ago, I decided to go on a nine-day cleanse—just to see what would happen—so I basically drank my food for a week. I threw a bunch of raw vegetables in the blender with some water and some protein powder, and I loved every disgusting minute of it. I lost ten pounds, five of them on the first two days (even though my goal wasn't actually to lose weight at that point.) And on day seven, I went in for my very first colonic. Here's what happened:

An overweight Russian lady with a sense of humor shoved a probe up my ass while I lay there on my side, naked. Fortunately, it wasn't *that* big and, aside from the initial intrusiveness—which made it near impossible for me to refrain from clenching—it wasn't that unbearable. I just took a few deep breaths and kept reminding myself that this was good for my body. She then proceeded to fill my colon with warm water until I felt like I was going to shit myself, turned off the flow of water, and then reversed it. This went on for about twenty minutes while she massaged different parts of my midsection.

Things started to come out. It was all directed through this clear plastic tube, which was part of this big metal machine hanging on the wall. I told her I wasn't interested in looking at it. "Everyone says that," she said. "But when it comes, you're going to change your mind." She was right—a few minutes later, I was glued to that thing like it was the season finale of *The Sopranos*.

"You see that?" she said, pointing to the tube. "That is yeast. You are eating too much bread, or drinking too much coffee."

"No, I'm not really into bread," I told her, "and I never drink coffee."

"What about alcohol? You drink alcohol?"

"Fuck, yeah," I said. "Every day."

"That is yeast that's stuck in your colon," she said again. "You drink too much alcohol. You need to stop that."

This lady was like a psychic! Not only did she know that I drank too much (without me having to tell her), she also said I was eating too many spicy foods—which is true, I put hot sauce on my goddamn oatmeal. She filled me up and flushed me out about seven or eight more times, and then sent me to the restroom to release anything else that might have been left. Then I got dressed and paid out front. To make a long story short, I basically paid $115 to take the biggest shit of my life . . . *times fourteen*. The experience was comparable to going to the chiropractor—an unnecessary luxury, in my opinion, but totally worth it every now and then. Even though it was one of the most uncomfortable hours of my life thus far, I will definitely be going back for more. *Eventually.*

Afterward, I felt like I was flying around Manhattan with a giant red "S" painted on my shirt. My skin looked incredible. Everywhere I went, people kept asking me if I'd done something different with my hair. "There's something different about you, dude. You look amazing." I just smiled and said "Thank you," which was a lot more comfortable than telling people I'd eaten nothing but spinach and kale all week, and then had a tube shoved up my ass.

Here's the thing, you don't have to get a colonic to look sexy (even though flushing out all that shit *will* make you feel like a rock star). Having my colon cleansed by a trained professional was just something I chose to do for me, because I wanted to see what all the fuss was about.

In case you haven't figured it out yet, the Drunk Diet isn't really a *diet* at all, at least not in the traditional sense. Personally, I think any "diet" plan that requires you to buy a shitload of prepackaged, frozen food, or to pay monthly dues to attend meetings, or to swallow a pill before every meal seems like a load of crap. It seems to me that what most of these fee-based diets are really selling is the idea that weight loss is easy, or that the only way to lose weight is to pay somebody to help you do it. You will never catch me standing in line to weigh myself in front of a room full of strangers—and I sure as fuck wouldn't pay for the privilege.

The Drunk Diet is a *lifestyle*. It's about making changes, setting goals, achieving those goals, and then setting new ones. It's about knowing that you are smart enough to make your own decisions about what you should and should not eat. If someone tells you that you're "doing it wrong," or that "you'll never lose weight that way," tell them to go fuck themselves. I decided to give up cheese and diet soda and get a colonic; you've got to decide what's right for you.

Of course, I realize that you might need some help deciding what's right for you—after all, you bought this book. I've spent the last three chapters talking about how I learned to stop eating crap. So now let's talk about how to turn *your* everyday shitty diet into a diet fit for a champion.

BREAKFAST

It's true, breakfast is the most important meal of the day: If Mrs. Caveman had fed Mr. Caveman cheeseburgers and French fries every morning, he would've been too tired and rundown to go hunt the cow in the first place. Without the cow you have no cheeseburger, and the cave family would've starved to death. I prefer to make breakfast my biggest meal of the day and to eat it early, which lets my body know that it's time to wake up and start doing shit.

If you normally start your day with a bowl of cereal and milk, it's time to switch. Most cereals—even the so-called "healthy" ones—are loaded with fat and sugar; some cereals have as much sugar as a can of soda. And don't think you're making a wise decision by purchasing the box marked "low sugar," either. Low-sugar cereals often have sky-high sodium content, to account for the fact that they taste like shit. A better option is oatmeal and water. You want 100 percent rolled oats, not that instant stuff with all the fake sugar and crap. (I get the big can of Quaker Oats, mostly because my dad looks just like Wilford Brimley.) Oatmeal is packed with good carbs to get you through the day, and a decent amount of fiber to help you take a healthy shit. Microwave the oatmeal for two minutes and then add some blueberries on top. If you don't care for the taste, mix in a dash of brown sugar. I prefer to put a couple tablespoons of chocolate whey protein on mine.

Another option: Egg whites, egg whites, egg whites! If you usually have eggs in the morning, that's great! I say, keep the whites, lose the yolks. Check this out:

EGG YOLKS	EGG WHITES	THE WHOLE ENCHILADA
Calories: 55	Calories: 17	Calories: 72
Fat: 4.5g	Fat: 0.1g	Fat: 4.6g
Saturated Fat: 1.6g	Saturated Fat: 0.0g	Saturated Fat: 1.6g
Cholesterol: 210mg	Cholesterol: 0.0mg	Cholesterol: 210mg
Protein: 2.7g	Protein: 5g	Protein: 7.7g

One yolk has 75 percent of your entire day's worth of cholesterol, as well as a lot of calories and fat. But guess what? An egg white omelet tastes exactly the same as a regular omelet, and has almost as much protein. Keep this up for a week, and you'll have no interest in the yolks ever again; they're worthless fat that you just don't need . . . unless you're a marathon runner. If you're running five miles or more a day, by all means, go ahead and eat a yolk or two. Otherwise, eliminate the yolks until you reach your goal weight, then mix in one yolk for every three to four eggs you eat.

I find that men in general have a hard time eating just the whites. They feel emasculated. The one time I got my father to make me scrambled whites on a fishing trip it turned into a huge screaming match because he thought I was being a pussy. Well, Pops, I'm in incredible shape and you're 100 pounds overweight, so I think I'll stick with my routine.

I always have at least a dozen fresh and a dozen hard-boiled eggs in my fridge. In fact, it's not uncommon for me to have four-dozen eggs in there at any given time. I usually eat five to six hard-boiled whites per day. They're great as a snack or even as a meal in the morning. Three or four egg whites prepared however you prefer (try Lüc Foo-Young, recipe on page 223) with a little bit of oatmeal, is the perfect breakfast. When you get bored with that, try making yourself some Rocket Fuel, or slapping a little bit of all-natural peanut butter on some whole-grain or live-grain toast.

What the fuck is an *Egg White?*

First of all, the yellow part of an egg—the yolk—is not an unborn chicken. The eggs you buy at the store are generally unfertilized, which means the hen wasn't knocked up when she laid it. But if there *were* a chick growing in the egg, the yolk is what it would eat, which is why yolks are full of fat and protein; they exist to turn baby chicks into fat hens. The "white"—the clear liquid that surrounds the yolk—turns white when you cook it, it has very little fat, and eating it will turn you into a badass. However, there was a day, not all that long ago, when I had no idea how to separate an egg. So for all you morons out there, here's how it's done:

Get a bowl and an egg. Crack the egg on the counter (don't be afraid to give it a good whack, now's not the time to be a pussy), and then carefully pull the shell apart so that you're holding two halves, one in each hand. Now, holding the egg over the bowl, gently pass the yellow yolk from one half of the shell to the other, letting the white part drip down into the bowl. Don't break the yolk—that'll screw everything up. When all the white has made it into the bowl, you should be left holding a half-broken shell with just the little yellow yolk inside. Throw that fucker away.

LUNCH

If we're being honest, I'm pretty fucking boring when it comes to food. I usually eat the same shit day in and day out, because then I don't have to waste a bunch of time trying to figure out if some new food is good for me, or if it's going to fuck up my diet, or wondering if it will fit in my steamer. In fact, I mainly eat the same types of foods I always ate, even when I was fat—stuff that I recognize and that I'm comfortable with. I just figured out how to turn my old bad-for-you meals into healthier, sexier versions. I ditched the fried starches, fortified pastas, and breads, and try to stick with the kinds of unprocessed foods our bodies were meant to eat, not the crap that's been created in a laboratory to make major corporations even more money than they already have. So when it comes time for lunch (or any meal, really), just think about what you'd normally eat on a daily basis and what simple changes you can implement to make it healthier and sexier.

For example, if you usually eat a turkey sandwich on a roll with mayonnaise and Swiss cheese for lunch, that's fine—just lose the roll, the cheese, and the mayonnaise. Try making your sandwich at home using live-grain or Bible bread, low-sodium turkey breast, and mustard. Add some lettuce and tomato, sprinkle on some pepper, and add a dash of hot sauce, and you've lost all the bad calories and unhealthy fats that you've been eating at lunch for years.

Speaking of lunch meats, did you know they're made of the same protein as the protein in your muscles? If you want your muscles to grow (and heal themselves before your next workout), you have to feed them protein. Unfortunately, choosing lunch meats that aren't shot full of salt, citric acid, and other crap to keep it "fresher" is tricky; most of the stuff at the store isn't really turkey at all, it's turkey with "extras." In general, it's best to buy the stuff from small, local companies rather than the big shitty corporations, but here's some advice: If you're shopping at the local Sack and Save, buy your meat from the deli counter; it'll be healthier than the prepackaged cold cuts they sell over by the pickles. If you have access to a healthier grocery store, like a Trader Joe's (I love those guys, by the way), then you can buy your lunch meat in the packages. I know, it gets confusing as fuck. The main thing to remember is: the fewer ingredients the better. After all, we're just trying to put some turkey on a sandwich. What are those twenty-eight other ingredients doing jammed in there? And how the fuck did they get them in there anyway? And *why?* You should start asking your food questions; if your food can't come up with a good answer, don't eat it.

What the fuck is *Bible Bread*?
Bible bread: A type of bread made from whole grains that have been allowed to germinate; inspired by a "recipe" in the Old Testament

So, white bread—the soft, fluffy stuff your mom probably used for your peanut butter and jelly sandwiches—is basically shit, because it's made with refined flour, which means the bran and wheat germ have been removed, along with all the fiber and nutrients that make grains good for you in the first place. Bible bread, on the other hand (also known as live-grain or sprouted grain bread), is made with grains that have been allowed to sprout; it's better for you, since it's loaded with vitamins, and you should eat it. Check out Ezekiel 4:9, which you can find at grocery stores like Whole Foods and Trader Joe's. Wherever you buy your bread, remember: the fewer ingredients on the label the better.

DINNER

If you stick to your guns at breakfast and lunch, it's okay to be a little more relaxed at dinner. Of course, that doesn't mean you can have a huge plate of Chicken Alfredo with two slices of white bread and a huge baked potato, and then wash that down with five beers and go back for seconds. It means having some lean protein, lots of vegetables, and—maybe—a few unrefined carbs, like a small serving of whole-wheat pasta or brown rice. Personally, I tend to stick with baked chicken or fish, broccoli, asparagus, or some other green vegetable, a slice of Bible bread, and sometimes a few steamed shrimp on the side. Try to avoid making your main course a pasta dish (even if it's whole-wheat pasta)—as we've already discussed, it's best to eat most of your carbs earlier in the day—unless you're planning on going on a long run or participating in some kind of serious sporting event the next morning. (You can find a few additional suggestions for dinner in the Recipes section at the back of this book).

I can't say this enough: Whatever you're eating, the main thing is not to *overeat*, and to allow yourself a few hours between your last meal of the day and bedtime. How do you do this? Willpower. You are stronger than the pasta. You are the master of your own universe. You don't need a meatball to make you happy; being sexy and healthy will make you happier than a colon full of calories, anyway. Look, I would never ask anyone—especially myself—to give up meatballs *entirely* (or bread, or pasta, or Sloppy Joes), but for Christ's sake, don't include them in your regular meal rotation. Sometimes even I have to force my brain to shut off the feeling of hunger after my evening meal—instead of my stomach telling my brain that it's full, I use my brain to tell my stomach that I'm finished.

PORTION CONTROL

I still consider myself a fat person, much like a drug addict considers himself to be a drug addict even when he isn't using anymore. I'm still a fat person—I'm just in a skinny person's body (and I'm determined to keep in that way). Still, one of my biggest problems is portion size. Even though I'd buy only healthy foods from the grocery store—fruits, veggies, chicken breast—I'd still try to eat it all at once. I'd make myself a sandwich for lunch, and then take a pound of grapes to the couch with me, along with an entire bag of Sun Chips and a large container of sliced cantaloupe. If you eat a whole pound of grapes and half a cantaloupe with your sandwich, and wash that down with a bag of chips, you're not going to lose any weight.

Let's say you bought a pound of low-sodium turkey breast. One pound of meat should make four sandwiches—four ounces of meat per sandwich. Eat any more than that and you're overeating. I even go to the extent of taking the turkey out of the deli bag and putting it into three separate sandwich bags. That way I know it's three separate meals later on, and that's that. End of story. Put the other portion on a plate with a couple of slices of cantaloupe and a handful of grapes, and that's lunch. Leave the rest of the grapes in the fridge so you won't be tempted to eat the whole damn bag.

Once a week, I make what's known as Lüc's Surprise (read the recipe on page 226), which is kind of like turkey chili. I love the shit out of it. I'll buy a big package of ground turkey (it's better for you than beef), green, yellow, and red bell peppers, a package of mushrooms, an onion, and a small jar of organic marinara sauce with no salt added. I'll sauté the vegetables in just a little bit of olive oil, brown the turkey, and then throw everything in a big pan with the marinara. Sometimes, I'll add whole-wheat pasta or black beans. I also like to throw some garlic and spices in there, whatever I happen to pass by in the grocery store that looks like it'll work with Lüc's Surprise. This makes about five meals. I'll eat one serving right after I cook it, then I'll put the rest in the fridge in four separate plastic containers. That way I know for certain that it's four separate meals. If I open one of those containers, that's a meal. There's no cheating allowed. Finishing one and then opening another container and nibbling at it is not an option. Only a fat person with a weight problem would do something like that.

You hear all this crap about how eating six small meals per day will keep your metabolism in check. While that's actually true, in order to eat six meals a day without raising your daily caloric intake, each meal has to be so small that, after you eat it, you'll feel like you didn't eat anything. Twenty minutes later, you'll be standing in front of the fridge in your underwear, dripping spaghetti sauce all over the floor.

I shoot for around four meals per day; that keeps my metabolism running like a high-performance hot rod. It's what works best for me personally, and keeps me from overeating. One of my four meals is a shake, which I usually drink right after the gym or after a run, but sometimes I mix things up and have one for breakfast instead. You can't let your body catch on and predict what you're going to put into it, or it'll figure out ways to store even healthy foods as fat.

SNACKING

Snacking is important. The longer you wait to eat between meals, the more your body thinks you are depriving it of what it needs to run, so it starts storing as much fat as possible. The closer the tank gets to empty, the more the machine tries to hold on to the fuel. If you keep putting food in, however, your body will relax. *Okay*, your body thinks to itself, *there's more coming in. Let's get rid of that last load.* Let's say you eat 2,000 calories a day like a normal person should, but you eat 1,000 calories in the early afternoon and 1,000 calories late at night. That's way too much time between meals, and you're confusing your body. It feels full and then it feels starved, so it stores as much as possible (as fat).

This also occurs if you don't eat until several hours after waking up. By the time you wake up in the morning, it's probably been anywhere from nine to twelve hours since you last had anything to eat, depending on when you had dinner and how late you slept. If you then wait another three or four hours after getting up to eat breakfast—or, technically, lunch—your body still thinks it's in "sleep mode"; it's going to hold on to that next meal for as long as possible. And naturally, if your body felt starved in the morning, you're going to wind up hungrier and eat more than you should in the afternoon. You'll also be more likely to eat crap that will make you fat. If you eat right when you wake up, and then again two or three hours later, and then again three hours after that, your body will just take the vitamins and nutrients it needs, and dump the rest.

Got it? It's okay to snack. It is not okay, however, to have a "power bar." Power bars are glorified candy bars. Yes, they're filled with protein and energy to get you through the day, but they're also filled with sugar, preservatives, and high fructose corn syrup. It's all marketing, and people are stupid—they'll buy anything they see on TV.

The only time I will allow myself to have a prepackaged bar of mystery ingredients is if I'm in the middle of a twenty-five-mile bike ride, and I suddenly realize that I haven't eaten in five hours. Then yes, I'll stop and get myself an energy bar. But that's really the only time these candy bars come in handy.

Don't eat them every day as a snack. I think a lot of people are actually stopping off to get themselves a protein bar mid-afternoon, feeling proud and thinking this little chocolate-covered devil is improving their overall health. How could anyone possibly think that something covered in chocolate is good for you? Snickers bars are also covered with chocolate; are you under the impression that a Snickers bar is going to do wonders for your waistline?

When I get a craving for a snack, I eat a can of tuna. I buy the can labeled INGREDIENTS: TUNA, WATER. There's only one type on the shelf in my grocery store that says that. The rest of them are packed full of preservatives and a shitload of salt and other crap that your body doesn't need to have flowing through its bloodstream. Eat your tuna with some pepper and bit of hot sauce or mustard, and have a piece of fruit, like a banana or an apple.

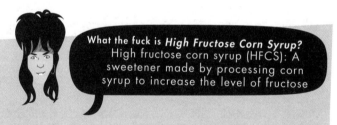

What the fuck is *High Fructose Corn Syrup?* High fructose corn syrup (HFCS): A sweetener made by processing corn syrup to increase the level of fructose

In the 1970s the price of natural cane sugar (aka sucrose) went through the roof, making the cost of foods that were made with natural sugar almost unaffordable. Around the same time a bunch of scientists got together and figured out a way to turn corn, one of America's agricultural staples, into a sugar substitute. Americans love cheap shit, and soon HFCS was in *everything*. For example, since natural cane sugar had been the most expensive ingredient in soda, all the major soda companies

(continued)

quickly switched. (These days, the profit margin on soda is just fucking outrageous, since the shit costs next to nothing to make.)

When HFCS was first introduced, no one really questioned what the effects might be of consuming so much fructose. I mean, fruit has fructose, just like a can of soda. But a piece of fruit also has vitamins and fiber and, of course, fruit also comes from nature—it was a gift from our creator, whether that's God, Allah, or Ozzy; it was given to mankind. But, just like a lot of things, mankind fucked it all up. (To give you a better idea of the difference between natural fructose and HFCS, a 20oz. bottle of soda has about five or six times the amount of fructose as an average-sized apple, and apples are actually relatively high in fructose compare to other fruits.)

It took thirty years for the American public to figure out that HFCS might be bad for them, and the word of mouth has been bad for business; consumption of HFCS has dropped year over year for the last decade. That's why the Corn Refiners Association is currently campaigning to change the name of "High Fructose Corn Syrup" to "Corn Sugar." Their argument is that whether it comes from sugar cane or corn, it's still sugar and your body can't tell the difference. Bullshit.

Studies have indicated that fructose may raise your blood pressure, increase your triglycerides (a type of fat), and may even cause weight gain. Also, fructose doesn't trigger insulin or leptin production—the hormone that makes you feel full—so you may feel hungry even if you've already put down several hundred calories. If those calories had come from something that wasn't produced by assholes, your stomach would know to tell you that it's full and it's time to put down the fork. Instead, you just keep eating. What the fuck.

SPORTS DRINKS ARE FOR PROFESSIONAL ATHLETES

So, you've gotta wash all this food down with something, and it can't always be beer. When I'm not drinking alcohol, I go for a straight shot of water—and that's it. There is no reason in hell that any normal human being should drink Gatorade or Vitamin Water. It's sugar water. You know those flavored sugar packets you mix with water, the kind with the big fat red pitcher as a mascot? Sports drinks are made of the same shit, only they're packaged for individual sale and promoted by well-compensated professional athletes. If you happen to be a professional football player burning 4,000 calories a day in the hot sun, then by all means, have yourself a sports drink. But if you go to the gym for an hour a few times a week, drinking anything other than water while you're working out is ridiculous. The only time I drink Gatorade is if I'm literally running a marathon, or doing a 100+ mile bike ride. And even then I fill my bottle with half Gatorade and half water. A regular-size Gatorade has 28 grams of sugar; grab a big one and we're looking at 56 fucking grams. If you drink more than a couple of Gatorades, you can feel the sugar building up on your teeth. Imagine what it's doing on the inside of your body.

This isn't to say that I think Gatorade is a bad product; I just think people are stupid and brainwashed, and drink it inappropriately. In fact, when you're *really* pushing yourself, you're gonna need all the Gatorade you can possibly get. For example, the human bloodstream stores around 2,000 calories when it's fully fueled. To run a marathon, you'll need anywhere from 2,600–3,000 calories. So, obviously, you're going to run out of calories at some point—that's why long-distance running is so damn difficult, and why it's necessary to keep replenishing.

If you were to drink a sports drink every ten minutes while sitting on your ass behind a desk all day, your bladder would explode. When you run for four hours straight and drink something every 1.5 miles, on the other hand, you still might not have to piss for hours after you've finished the race. That's because you're burning up those calories, and your body is using the water to replenish the cells and keep them alive.

Water, by the way, is probably the most important element in a healthy diet (and a sexy body)—especially when you drink as much alcohol as I do. It's almost like changing the oil in your car; the longer the oil sits in your engine, the more filled with shit (like metal fragments and dirt) it becomes. Same idea when it comes to staying hydrated. If your piss is dark yellow, then it has a lot of waste in it and you're not drinking enough water. You don't really need to worry about drinking "eight glasses a day," but your piss should be damn near clear pretty much all the time.

What the fuck is an *Electrolyte?*
Electrolytes: Electrically charged substances that regulate metabolism and fluids

Basically, what all that crap means is that electrolytes—including sodium, chloride, and potassium—all conduct . . . wait for it . . . *electricity.* Your body needs them because they carry electrical impulses from cell to cell, which is what keeps your nerves, muscles, and brain functioning. When you're doing a vigorous activity for a long period of time, however, such as running—and we're talking at least five miles here, not once around the block—your body starts to lose a lot of those electrolytes through sweat. If you sweat *too* much, you'll also start to lose some of your energy, strength, and endurance. (By the way, sodium + chloride = salt, which is why your sweat tastes salty.)

Back in the 1960s, the football coaches at the University of Florida realized that their athletes were getting seriously dehydrated and run down, and they needed something other than juice to fuel them up. "Gatorade," which is basically just sugar water with a little added sodium chloride, was born. Unless you're playing a four-hour football game and burning off a thousand calories in the process, you're better off eating a banana (for its potassium) and drinking some tap water. Even the football players have caught on—next time you're getting drunk on a Sunday afternoon, stuffing your face with burritos, check the sideline. With the right camera angle, you'll see a shitload of bananas down there.

EATING WITH A HANGOVER

This is tough. This is very tough. After a night of heavy drinking, your head hurts, you're sweating, and your whole body hates you. This is your body's way of saying, *Fuck you! Why did you do this to me?* And on a morning like that, there's nothing that sounds better than a cheeseburger with French fries. Why does one have such a strong desire to eat shit the day after getting wasted? Because your body is still breaking down all those toxins from the booze, and your liver is still trying to filter out all the crap you put into it the night before. Sweating occurs, too, because it helps pump all that crap out through your pores. That's why alcoholics always smell like booze, even if they haven't had a drink for several hours. Their faces might also turn bright red, flushed, and blotchy, because the blood cells are working overtime. It's called "alcohol flush reaction." I've seen many people with this condition. You know, like your Uncle Jim. We all have one or two alcoholics in our extended families.

Eating fatty foods coats the stomach, slows the absorption of alcohol into the bloodstream, and generally makes it easier for your body to deal. That's why, when you wake up after a night of drinking your face off, you immediately think of Mexican food. Or, if you're really dying, you might crack open another beer or have a Bloody Mary. (Bloody Marys, by the way, are amazing—the tomato juice has vitamins, the spice helps you sweat out the booze, and the relatively small amount of alcohol makes your liver slow down the process that's making you feel like shit. Your liver likes to wait until you're done filling it with crap before it really begins attacking those toxins and removing them from your body. If you put in a few more toxins, it slows down the attack.)

My perfect hangover combination: eggs and bananas. Eggs contain a large amount of cysteine, the substance that breaks down the hangover-causing toxin acetaldehyde (a substance that is produced when your liver tries to metabolize all the alcohol you drank). Therefore, eggs can potentially help mop up any leftover toxins. Your body is also depleted of potassium during the after-drinking cleansing process. And it's true what they say about bananas, they are quite possibly the world's simplest, greatest food—one banana has about 15 percent of your daily potassium.

A western omelet with a banana is the healthiest restaurant option when you have a hangover. Do not order the home fries or hash browns! Your body is going to be begging you for the starchy, fatty goodness of those oily potatoes to help it process all that crap pumping through your veins, but you must resist. I find the very best cure for a terrible hangover is actually exercise. I lace up my shoes, get out there, and run a mile or two. Hell, walk if you have to. Just get out there. You'll sweat all that crap out in no time, and you won't be consuming all those calories and saturated fats from fried meat and potatoes.

DON'T BE A "DRUNKOREXIC"

Here's the poop . . . right around the time I first started my diet, I talked to a go-go dancer friend of mine about how she keeps herself so thin. She told me that the only way she ever lost any weight was if she starved herself. That was good enough for me—let's give it a try! I immediately started depriving myself of food on a fairly regular basis. On the nights that I worked (about three nights a week), I'd order a healthy breakfast or lunch, usually something with chicken and brown rice, and then on my way to work, I'd pick up a piece of fruit from the deli and two giant bottles of water. For dinner, I'd get drunk. I did that for longer than I care to admit. This is called "drunk-orexia," and it's not good for you. But back then, I didn't give a shit if I was healthy or not. I was losing weight and getting re-sults. When you want something bad enough, you'll do what-ever the fuck it takes to make it happen. I wanted to be skinny, so I stopped eating.

When you starve yourself, your stomach sort of becomes its own person; it's no longer part of your body. It has its own personality. And on those nights when I wouldn't eat for twelve hours, my stomach would start talking to me. I could feel it turning around inside itself. It was like my stomach was going through some kind of deep emotional struggle—it was depressed because it was being punished. I was punishing it because I was unhappy with it. And I was unhappy with it be-cause I didn't have washboard abs. Alcohol helped numb this internal struggle. I was drinking straight vodka just so I wouldn't feel hungry.

Okay, so when I say I "starved myself," it's not like I wasn't eating in some kind of weird I-hate-my-father-so-I-starve-myself kind of way; it's really just my wiseass way of saying I didn't eat as much as I normally would. I was still taking in about 1,000–1,500 calories a day in food, and another 1,000 calories at night in booze. So technically, I was getting the recommended 2,000–2,500 calories per day, but since half of those calories came from alcohol, they served no nutritional value.

I'll be honest, though, there was a period of time where I took things too far, as I do with most things in my life. I liked feeling empty. It made me feel good about myself. It made me happy, because I knew I was going to wake up in the morning and step on the scale and like what I saw. On those three nights a week that I drank instead of eating, I was pretty much guaranteed to drop a pound. I'd put myself to sleep thinking about what I was going to eat for lunch, and in the morning I was so excited to weigh in, I was like an eight-year-old on Christmas morning.

And then it got to the point where I was too damn skinny. At my lowest, I dropped down to 158 pounds. At 6'3" this was not a good look. Later on, I got my shit together and figured out how to gain muscle and start getting shredded without looking like a meathead.

Here's what a lot of doctors and other assholes won't tell you: It is totally acceptable to skip a meal every once in a while, particularly when it's the last meal of the day, and your first two meals were a little bigger than they should have been. I mean, if it's eleven o'clock at night and you haven't eaten dinner yet, just go to bed! Chances are you already had enough calories during the day, anyway. It is in no way acceptable, however, to skip meals on purpose, or worse, to plan to skip meals in advance. Skipping a meal is like anything in life; it's best enjoyed in moderation. When skipping meals becomes a regular thing, you've got a serious problem on your hands. Don't try this at home, kids. Learn from my mistakes. (Trust me, sometimes it's better to learn from someone else's mistakes than it is to make your own.)

RESTAURANTS—THE DOWNFALL OF MAN

I rarely eat out anymore. It's just so hard to eat healthy in a restaurant. It's like being a drug addict. If you were a cokehead and you set foot in a bar that you used to do a lot of coke in, chances are you're going to be tempted to call your dealer. For me, the restaurant is the dealer. The pineapple-fried rice is the drug. When I do go to a restaurant, I make sure it's not one I used to go to when I was a fatty. It will trigger the memories of eating like shit, and I'd prefer to avoid that completely.

To be honest with you, I don't really like going out to eat— I've always had anxiety when it comes to restaurants. When I was fat, I'd feel almost guilty eating in public, and I didn't want to be anywhere where people could watch me eat. I was convinced that other people were secretly whispering about me: "Why the fuck is that fat ass eating those mashed potatoes? Maybe if he wasn't eating right now he wouldn't look so disgusting." It's not a good feeling. In fact, I should probably see a psychologist.

To me, eating at restaurants has always been more like a race to finish; I always want to get it over with as soon as possible. I fucking hate the crowds of people. Then there's the waiting to order, waiting for my food, waiting to pay, waiting for a refill. It's just a shitload of waiting. I don't have the patience. Not to mention the fact that I feel weird having some stranger—who probably just jerked off, using the hand that's touching my plate—bring me food like I'm some kind of king who expects things from people who are lesser then them. Clearly, serving people food and booze for ten years has turned me into some kind of jaded fuck. But I can't help it—I know what the waiters and bartenders are thinking, and I simply cannot relax and enjoy myself with this entire caste system unfolding before my eyes. Don't get me wrong, I still love to go out with the boys for steaks once a month, but I tip my ass off in order to avoid these feelings of shame and guilt.

I'm perfectly aware that not all of you are as fucking crazy as I am, but I'm quite certain that a large number of people can relate to being uncomfortable with being watched while eating. (Even though, in reality, no one is really watching you. I mean, who would want to watch a total stranger eat? That would make *them* the crazy person, not you.) Unfortunately, that feeling that people are staring at you thinking, "why is that fatty eating" is one of those feelings that can drive a person to anorexia. That is, obviously, not a good thing. But at least this gives me something to work on every day.

When you're trying to lose weight, I think it's best to just switch to a whole new set of restaurants. If you had a favorite place to go eat meat loaf, for example, it's going to be difficult to continue going to that same place and not ordering the meat loaf. Even if you do talk yourself into ordering a salad, you're just going to be fantasizing about the fucking meat loaf for the whole hour and a half that you're at the restaurant. Don't do that to yourself—just go somewhere else. Even if the new place *has* meat loaf, your taste buds won't be reminding you of that if the only thing you've ever ordered at said new place is a chicken salad with the dressing on the side.

LIFE HAPPENS—VACATIONS AND HOLIDAY EATING

You know that feeling you get every time you're on vacation? The feeling that you're doing something wrong, the feeling that life is really going to suck as soon as you go back to reality? That feeling is called guilt, and it *is* possible to overcome.

Even after completely changing my eating habits, every time I went on vacation (or out of town for any reason), I would totally blow it—any time you get out of your daily routine it's just so easy to want to reward yourself by eating fatty, fried, delicious food for a change. But then I'd come back home eight pounds heavier and bloated as hell. It also doesn't help that whenever I'm on vacation, I start drinking at noon. And I usually don't stop until it's time for bed.

Here's the harsh reality that nobody wants to admit: your brain and your taste buds all know that you're on vacation. Your fat cells, however, do not. They don't give a flying fuck whether you're relaxing on the beach or sitting behind a desk in a tiny cubicle pushing papers. I've fucked up more than a few times while on vacation, and I decided that it's better to give you some suggestions for not fucking up, rather than just telling you more stories about how I fucked up. Of course, none of this will apply to you if you're used to eating McDonalds every day, because you can find a McDonalds in every part of the world . . . except for maybe the Arctic Circle.

1. Plan Ahead—Mentally *and* Emotionally.

On your flight to wherever the hell you're going, be aware of what you are getting yourself into. Be aware that there will be temptation on every corner, and that you will be much more tempted to give into it due to the fact that you're no longer just living out your usual daily routine. Even before getting on the flight, get online and do some research on the area you're headed to. What kinds of food do they eat over there, what are those foods made of, and so on. People in certain parts of the world actually eat a very healthy diet, and people in other parts eat like shit. Know what you're getting into before you get yourself into it. Which leads me to suggestion number two . . .

2. Just Because You've Heard of It Doesn't Mean You Should Eat It.

You walk (or drive) by Dunkin' Donuts on your way to work every single day, yet you rarely stop in. But when you're on vacation—especially in a foreign country—it's really easy to get intimidated by food you've never heard of, especially if you can't even pronounce it. This does not make it okay to eat a Quarter Pounder with cheese. You've heard of a grocery store, haven't you? Unless you're on a deserted island (and God bless you if you are), there are grocery stores in every inhabited place in the world. Take an hour out of your first day to find the nearest grocery store and buy the foods that you're familiar with and that you eat on a regular basis. If you buy a bag of apples, it'll last you a whole week, even without refrigeration. And if you can manage to get yourself a room with a mini fridge, pick yourself up some lunch meat and some decent bread to make sandwiches.

3. Work Out on Vacation!

Here's the thing, most of us would rather kill ourselves than go to the gym while on vacation, but that makes no sense whatsoever. I'm going to prove it to you.

First, nearly all hotels have gyms these days, unless you're staying in a $35-a-night special; then you'll need to bring your own dumbbells. You know all those excuses people make about working out? *I'm too tired, I don't have enough time, I had to take the kids to school, I had a deadline at work.* Well, none of those things apply . . . because *you're on fucking vacation.* In fact, vacation is a great time to bust out a PR because you're so damn rested and stress-free. Granted, not all vacations are stress-free, especially if you're taking the kids to see the Eiffel tower. But if you ask me, there's no point in even taking a stressful vacation. Take your significant other and sneak off on a nice little four-day getaway to the Caribbean, and take your running shoes with you. There is nothing better than leaving the snow-covered brutal cold of the Northeast for a quick two-and-a-half hour flight to the Caribbean in the middle of February. It's 75 degrees of pure bliss. Sleep for ten hours a night, wake up at sunrise, and put in a nice six-mile run. And the best part about running in the morning while on vacation is that you don't have to feel guilty about all those damn beers you're going to drink later on in the day.

What the fuck is a **PR?**
PR: Personal record

Yes, dumbass, it's when you do something better than you've ever done it before. You should be striving for this achievement more often. Trust me, you'll feel better about yourself.

4. Plan to Cheat.

This is what my inner monologue sounds like on vacation: *Now, what makes you think it's okay to eat pork-fried rice at the buffet twice a day when you're in Vegas? You wouldn't eat like that when you're at home, would you? What the fuck is wrong with you? By the time you get back to work on Monday, you're going to have a hell of a time fitting into your already skintight jeans.*

Don't do this to yourself. Don't drive yourself crazy. It's okay to splurge a little bit—you're on fucking vacation! Don't just go crazy the whole time you're away. For example, if you're planning to be on vacation for, say, four days, plan to indulge a little on *one* of those days. I prefer to save this for the last day. If I eat the good stuff the first day, I'm going to crave that crap for the rest of the trip. Save the fried catfish with rice and beans for the last day—it's much easier to do damage control on one night of shitty eating than an entire week of shitty eating.

5. Gaining Weight Is Not Convenient.

Speaking of that buffet, yes, it may be a hell of a lot easier to eat there than running to the grocery store while you're out of town. And yes, it may be a hell of a lot cheaper than eating at a fancy restaurant every night of your trip. But if you can't stay away from the roast beef and mashed potatoes—and I know you can't—then at least keep your fat ass away from the all-you-can-eat line. Because listen, it is a hell of a lot easier to walk a few blocks and pick up some fresh, healthy food at the store than it is to crash diet away the nine pounds you gained in a week.

6. The Holidays Are No Damn Holiday.

Okay, let's face it. The holidays are fucking stressful. If your Christmas is anything like it is with my family, it goes a little something like this:

Everyone is flying in from all parts of the country. Your brother is already drunk and calling you to meet the old gang at the corner bar. Your mother is an emotional roller coaster, trying to make sure everyone is happy and feeling like a total failure for absolutely no reason. Your father is between naps in his recliner, flipping back and forth between the football game and John Wayne movies. Your woman is stressed out, trying way too hard to be extra nice because she wants everyone to like her. Your brother's girlfriend is being way too nice because she wants *you* to like her. Your aunts and uncles are still talking to you like you're seventeen goddamn years old and trying to decide what college courses to take. And the whole damn time, all you want to do is drink as much whiskey as possible and wait for this fucking shit show to end—the day also known as January 2. Which, incidentally, is the day you find yourself ten pounds heavier than you'd like to be, and you're not even sure how it happened, other than the fact that you would rather have stuffed chocolate chip cookies into your mouth than tell the same fucking story about what-you've-been-doing-with-yourself, when really what you want to say is, *Well, I've been getting shit-drunk and eating too much to avoid talking to you people. It's not that I don't like you. I might even genuinely wish that you were a bigger part of my life. It's just that I know the second you walk away from me, somebody else with the same last name is going to walk up and ask me the same goddamn question. So, maybe if I shove more carrots covered in Ranch dip down my throat, people will think I'm too busy eating to chat.*

For the same reason, everyone drinks too much during the holidays. It's a stressful time of year. It's a time when we get together with family to love, laugh, fight, cry, and kick each other's asses. It's a time when we may regret that we don't call our grandmother as often as we should, and we hate to think about the fact that maybe this time next year, she won't be at the dinner table. It's enough to change that fucking Virgin Mary into a goddamn Bloody Mary.

My suggestion during the holidays is to put on your seat belt and fucking pray. I mean, it's not like you're going to be able to *skip* Christmas dinner, unless you're a fucking French Fry*, and you're not going to ask your mother to cook you a separate, healthy meal after she busted her ass in the kitchen for two days straight, unless you're an ungrateful asshole. Instead, keep your serving sizes to an absolute minimum, especially if you're eating more than one holiday meal with more than one side of the family. Limit yourself to one piece of turkey, one spoonful of stuffing, one spoonful of mashed potatoes, and skip the gravy. Keep reminding yourself that the less you eat now, the better January will be. And stay away from the eggnog, for Christ's sake. The main thing is to try not to be too hard on yourself come January if you've gained a few pounds. And get yourself right back in the gym, fat ass.

---

*French Fry (French-frī) N. Male or Female.
1. A person who eats small portions of shitty food.
2. Someone who orders a Philly cheesesteak with steak fries and then picks at it, leaving the majority of food on the plate; this person is generally a drunkorexic, and gets the majority of his or her calories from alcohol.

He's a French fry. We went to dinner last night and he didn't even touch the chicken; he only picked at the potatoes.

CHAPTER FIVE

The Booze or the Mirror?
A Never-ending Battle

LÜC'S LAW: DRUNK DOES NOT FEEL AS GOOD AS SEXY.

Next to Rock 'N' Roll, my hot rod Ginger, and a blonde with a big fat ass, I love beer more than anything in the world. All these things just go together; beer, blondes, and fast cars *are* Rock 'N' Roll. (Of course, don't mix the beer and the fast cars unless you're under the hood and not behind the wheel.) And it's perfectly okay to drink beer . . . if you only go out drinking one night a week. I, however, drink nearly every night. I party for a living, because it pays the bills pretty well (and because I'm good at it).

In fact, three nights a week, I know that I'm going to *have* to drink. Not necessarily get wasted, but it's impossible to be completely sober when you're bartending. I know for the rest of the world, it's hard to imagine getting drunk while you're at work (except for all you liquid lunch types—I know you can relate). But I work with drunk people for a living. In order to be surrounded by people who are drinking, I need to be in a similar state of mind. You wouldn't work at a guitar shop if you didn't love music, guitars, and being surrounded by other musicians, right? I mean, Guitar Center wouldn't even hire you in the first place. Back when I was working at the drum shop, I was more interested in getting off work and partying than I was in selling drums. So much so, that I would stay out partying until four A.M., sleep for a few hours, and go back to work the next day smelling like a whiskey distillery. That's no way to keep a job. Which is why I got into the bar business.

I love what I do for a living, but in order to be *good* at it, I've got to be in the mood to party. If you walk into a bar and go up and order your first round and the bartender is a dick, looks pissed off, or seems like he'd rather be anywhere else than behind that bar, chances are you won't stay for another round. But if the bartender looks cool, or maybe says something funny to you when you order, chances are you'll stick around. Maybe you'll even stay all night, especially if the place is filled with beautiful women and good-looking dudes. That's another reason I go to the gym and spend so much time on my hair, by the way—if I look good, good-looking people will hang out in my bar. Plus, I like to be surrounded by sexy people who care about how they look. In fact, I love it when one of my friends who has no money and no place to live comes up to me and shows me the new pants that he just blew $400 on. We might be broke, and we might not have a place to sleep tonight (unless we get laid), but at least we look cool as fuck.

Of course, bartending does have its downside. There is nothing worse than being stuck at work on a slow night and having to listen to a drunk person carrying on and on about the problems in their life. Not that this happens very much anymore; I rarely work on slow nights because I get the good shifts. (Hell, I get whatever shifts I want; I run the place.) But the bar can't always be packed, so sometimes I'm stuck listening to some drunk dumbass bitch about his girlfriend or how much he hates his job. I've got to stand there and pretend to give a shit. Meanwhile, I'm thinking to myself, *I went to the gym, ran four miles, and spent an hour doing my hair so I can hear about this jerk-off's problems for his shitty one-dollar tip?* Thank God it's not always like that. Most of the time, I'm so busy that I hardly have time to check my hair at all.

Anyway, after all that drinking and partying, I realized something: I was easily drinking as many as ten Budweisers in a night. Unfortunately, that equals 1,500 calories and over 100 grams of carbohydrates. Do that five nights a week, and you're up to 7,500 calories and 500 grams of carbs, on top of an already shitty diet of fried food. Jesus Christ! It's no wonder I used to be so damn fat.

Things changed, however, on a Tuesday in February 2009, just before midnight. I was at work, only a month into fooling around with my new diet and exercise plan, when something just clicked in my head. *That's it*, I thought. *This is the night I'm going to give up beer.* I wasn't going to give up beer forever, by the way, I just wanted to look incredible on the beach (and in bed), and I was ready to do whatever it took to get me to that point. Of course, giving up beer meant that I would also have to give up whiskey, one of my other favorite things. It's not that whiskey has a lot of carbs or anything (and there are fewer calories in a shot of whiskey than a whole bottle of beer), but drinking it makes me want to drink beer. The two just go together, like peas and carrots. In fact, my favorite combo is a shot of Jameson and a Budweiser, which in my bar is known as a Happy Meal. I'd top that off with a cigarette for dessert, and repeat . . . until either (a) I ran out of money, (b) I got too fucked up to remember my own name, or (c) someone called the cops.

So on this Tuesday night in February, I decided to pour

myself a carbohydrate-free vodka soda. After making thousands of these for customers (mostly female) at countless bars over the years (and never actually tasting one myself), I decided that this would be my new drink. And you know what? The vodka didn't make me bloated like the beer did. There was just one problem: I was drinking vodka sodas like water—because they taste like fucking water. Next thing you know, it's only been two hours and I'd be so goddamn hammered I could barely get my drunk ass into a cab to go home. Vodka sodas also made me tired. Drinking all of that alcohol (which is a depressant) without all the sugar and carbs that a beer has, just kind of ran me down. I started downing an energy drink every night at two A.M. just to keep the party going. I hated doing that—energy drinks, as we've already discussed, are filled with nasty shit—but if I wanted to make more money, I had to keep smiling and engaging; I couldn't be falling asleep behind the bar.

After a few weeks of drinking vodka sodas (and getting trashed way too fast), I had to find a way to slow it down, so I came up with the ingenious idea of the "half drink." I'd pour a single shot of vodka and two drinks' worth of soda water in a pint glass; that way, it was half as strong as a normal drink, and I could drink for twice as long. To give it a kick, I'd squeeze in a couple of limes and a lemon (vodka sodas have no flavor, so it doesn't matter how much soda water you put in there, it still tastes the same). On days that I wasn't working and I was drinking at someone else's bar, I'd attempt to order the "half drink," but I always ended up having to explain what it was I wanted—one shot of vodka, double the amount of soda water. Most of the time, I'd just get a dirty look from the bartender; they'd usually screw it up and just give me a double vodka soda, which totally backfires. First of all, it costs damn near $20 for a double anything at any regular bar in Manhattan. Second, it's like having two full-strength drinks that taste like water in your hand at a time; a one-way ticket to Wasted Town (on the express train). Eventually, I gave up trying to order the half drink altogether. It wasn't worth the hassle, and the last thing you want to do is piss off the bartender. We're very sensitive people, especially when it comes to someone ordering a drink that makes no sense. So I just started taking a bottle of water with me to every bar I went to and topping off my drink after every other sip. That way, one drink lasts twice as long, and keeps me from hitting the floor twice as fast.

Everything was going great with the no-beer thing. The weeks were flying by. I switched my vodka sodas to tequila sodas, which kept my energy up (and still had fewer calories and sugar than beer). And I was so proud, I started filling people in on my progress: "I haven't had a beer in three weeks, four weeks, five weeks, nine weeks . . ." I went nine fucking weeks without a beer! And then one night, I fell off the wagon. My boys and I had driven to Boston to see a friend play a show, and I found myself standing in a back alley double-fisting Coronas and smoking a joint (with a bottle of Crown Royal waiting for me backstage). I realized just how much I had missed beer, which was something I had managed to block from my brain for close to three long months. After that night, I was back to drinking beers again, but only on nights that I worked. However, I wasn't dropping the pounds like I had been, so I knew I would have to further curb how much I was drinking. I was going to have to let beer go, like an old friend that you love very much but whose life is moving on in a different direction.

My old friend was fat and sweaty; my new friend is ripped and has a better job.

From time to time, I would *think* about cracking open a Budweiser. I'd tell myself, *It's okay, go ahead and have a fucking beer. You deserve it. You work out six days a week and all these other assholes guzzling beer don't work out at all!* I'd struggle with the idea for twenty minutes or so, going over the positives and negatives. The thing is, I can't have just one; beers are like fucking Pringles. Once I crack that first one and pound it (because it tastes so goddamn good), I think it's okay to have another, and another, and another, and the next thing you know, it's six A.M. and I've had something like twelve beers and Lord knows how many shots of Jameson. These days I know that beer is my enemy. It's in the same category as chocolate cake; I just can't have it. This is a choice every man has to make. Do I want to drink beer, or do I want to wake up tomorrow and be excited to look in the mirror? Because if I drink beer, tomorrow won't be as good of a day as it would if I just stick to my half-tequila sodas and a couple of shots here and there.

I still love beer, of course. Beer is like a man's link to life; it's our reward for a hard day's work. But now I think of beer as something for special occasions, like Grandma's bread pudding. If you're the type of person that can have just one beer, okay, go for it. As for me, I usually allow myself one day every other week where I can drink beer and not feel bad about it. (Actually, I usually regret it the next day anyway, but the longer it's been since I've had one, the less remorse I feel.)

WINE IS FINE BUT LIQUOR IS QUICKER:
What to Drink and What to Avoid

Okay, here's the deal: All straight booze has about 100 calories per standard shot (about 1.5 ounces). And all hard liquors have zero carbs. When you order a cocktail, it generally comes in a 9 or 10-ounce glass; 1.5 ounces of that is booze, 2 to 3 ounces is the mixer, and the rest is ice. So, carbs and the majority of calories are, obviously, hidden in the mixers. Also, what goes on behind and underneath the bar is enough to make you swear off drinking for good. The entire mixing system is hooked up to what's known as "the gun." Let's say you order a Jack and Coke. This is how it goes down:

The bartender fills a glass with ice, pours in 1.5oz (give or take) of Jack Daniels, and fills the rest of the glass with 2–3oz (give or take) of Coke. What they don't tell you is that the "Coke" was really made at a guy named Louie's house in New Jersey and delivered to the bar on a truck eight months ago, then it sat in a corner collecting dust and getting covered in rat turds. See, the gun is connected to a tube, which is connected to a compressor, which pumps carbonated water into the Coke syrup. So when you order your Jack and Coke, the bartender is starting with a giant canister of fake soda that Louie made in his fucking bathtub for all you know, that syrup gets mixed with carbonated water, and then pumped through several feet of tubes that are most likely filled with mold and cockroach excrement. (I've worked in fancy bars and shithole bars, and none of them clean the lines. In fact, the best way to pass the health department inspection successfully, clean lines or not, is to pay off the cops.)

So not only are you pumping your body full of fake sugar, caffeine, and other man-made ingredients like coloring and dye,

(continued)

you're also pumping yourself full of whatever the fuck was in Louie's bathtub, whatever was in the tubes behind the bar, whatever mold and crap has built up inside the gun after twelve years of never having been cleaned, and hundreds of other people's germs from a wash sink that's had the same cold, filthy water in it for the past five and a half hours.

Okay, before I went off on that rant about how disgusting bars actually are, I had a really good point in there about how it is totally possible to get drunk without overloading yourself with calories. Stay away from mixed drinks with anything other than soda water and you're on the right track to a low-calorie buzz. If you love margaritas, just remind yourself that each one is more than 500 calories and you've probably got about seven more to go before you're feeling anything. Instead, try tequila and soda water with a couple squeezes of fresh lime—you won't hate yourself in the morning.

DRINK THIS

Vodka soda (100 calories, 0 carbs)

Whiskey soda (100 calories, 0 carbs)

Tequila soda with fresh lime
 (100 calories, 0 carbs)

Rum & Diet Coke
 (100 calories, 0 carbs)

Vodka martini (200 calories, 0 carbs,
 twice the booze)

FUCK THAT

Mai Tai (800+ calories)

Bloody Mary (1,500+mg salt)

Pina Colada (600+ calories, 60+ carbs)

Long Island Ice Tea (1,200+ calories,
 generally it's served as a double)

Margarita (500+ calories, 18g carbs)

THE NO-DRINKING EXPERIMENT

Look, I'm not going to lie. If I had stopped drinking for good, the whole process of losing weight and getting in shape probably would have been a lot easier. But not drinking is just not an option for me. I need alcohol to function at work, and I need it to function when I'm not at work and I'm blowing off steam. And there's not a damn thing wrong with that. As long as you're not waking up in the morning and pouring yourself a fucking cocktail, there's no reason you shouldn't be able to have a few glasses of wine—even when you're staying in and taking a night off. Every few months, if I feel like I've been partying a little too hard, I'll take a week off just to clear my head.

In fact, I stopped drinking completely for fourteen days about midway through my diet. Not to clear my head, but as an experiment—to see if I'd lose more weight by not drinking at all. I'd never gone two weeks without drinking in my life, not since I had my first beer in Lacy's white Corvette, but I figured it was about time I tried, and I wanted to see if it would jump-start my abs and really kick my ass into shape. I wanted to see, once and for all, if those doctors and other assholes were right, and I wanted to be able to tell you good people what happened. I'll tell you what happened. The first week, I lost about two pounds. The second week, I gained five pounds back and was worse off than when I started.

By the start of the second week, I found myself getting hungrier than normal. My body wanted a replacement for all of those calories and sugar that it was used to. If you're a heavy drinker and you suddenly stop drinking, you're going to start craving things like ice cream and chocolate cake, even if you don't typically eat things like that. By day ten, I was wandering around the frozen food section at the grocery store, looking for some sort of fake ice cream with no dairy. One night, I stopped off after a long run and bought a rotisserie chicken and a pint of sorbet. I got home and ate the entire fucking chicken and the whole fucking pint. This is no way to lose weight. I couldn't suppress my appetite, and I was craving sweets like you wouldn't believe. Now, I'm sure that if I had stuck with it, the cravings would have eventually gone away. But with my job and my lifestyle, I couldn't go another week just to find out. I was already losing my damn mind.

After fourteen days, I'd had enough. It wasn't working. The fifteenth day, the day I had planned to allow myself to start drinking again, was my bar's third anniversary party. (I planned it that way on purpose). This night is the one night of the year that I can go to my bar and get as wasted as I want. I can act like a fool in front of my employees and the customers and not even give a shit; it's my one free pass. But guess what? I still didn't overdo it. I have a hard time getting totally wasted in front of my employees, anyway. It's just bad for business. Before long, the bartenders will start thinking, *Lüc gets hammered all the time, I can drink as much as I want at work and no one will care.* Monkey see, monkey do. So when I'm working, I never get totally trashed. (I do that elsewhere, like at the bowling alley). I just stay loopy enough to have a good time and deal with the bullshit that gets thrown at me by drunk people. If I start feeling a little too drunk, I'll slow down and drink some water, and then I might have one more drink with the guys before it's time to close up and go home.

THE PARTY DOESN'T START 'TIL MIDNIGHT

If, like me, you make your living surrounded by all-you-can-drink booze (or just happen to drink a hell of a lot when you're out on the town), here's some advice: Don't start drinking 'til midnight. On nights that I'm working, I don't allow myself that first shot until the clock strikes twelve. And that's the way it's been for a while, actually, ever since the beginning of my days at the taco shop. It all started when one of the Mexicans got pissed at me. (This wasn't hard to accomplish; the Mexicans weren't too fond of us gringos to begin with.) This particular guy had done something stupid and gotten himself into some hot water with the boss. In order to save his own ass, he decided to say that I was getting sauced on the job. I went in for my shift one night and Kemo, the owner, asked me to come downstairs to his office. It was extremely rare that I ever even saw the guy, so I knew something was amiss.

Kemo sat down and told me a story about when he used to tend bar at a punk club on the Bowery. Every single night at midnight, he said, he'd go across the street to have a shot. That was always his first drink of the night. "If you start drinking at eight P.M. when your shift starts," he explained, "you have much more time to get hammered by four A.M. closing, which is unacceptable." So from that day on, I started going across the street to the bar where my buddy, Pauli Mohawk, worked, to have my first shot of the evening at midnight on the dot. I'd bring Pauli some fish tacos and guacamole as payment, and he'd give me a shot of whiskey and half a beer to wash it down. Then I'd pick up a couple of 40s at the deli on my way back to work. That way, I wasn't drinking the house beer at the taco shop, since Kemo kept an *incredibly* tight inventory and didn't want us drinking his stuff.

WINE IS THE NEW BEER

Wine is something I never really understood until fairly recently; before, I was too interested in Budweiser. And whenever I went to the liquor store to pick something up to keep around the house, it was a bottle of Irish or Canadian whiskey. Now it's a bottle of wine. I love to pick up a bottle of red on a night when I'm not bartending—I'll pop it open, put on some jazz, and cook myself a healthy dinner. Even if I'm headed to a rehearsal with a band or a party at a friend's house, I usually bring a bottle of wine with me. (And the guys are normally like,

"Shit, yeah! We've been drinking beer for six days straight, let's drink some wine to switch things up.")

The best thing about wine is that it's fairly easy on the waistline. Sure, wine has calories, but only about half the amount of calories in a beer—and twice the amount of alcohol, ounce for ounce. In fact, a whole bottle of wine has the same amount of calories as three-and-a-half Budweisers. There's a reason they don't call it a "wine gut."

Occasionally, I like to start with a white wine at dinner. Not only does it go better with a meal than beer, it shows your date you have class. I'm not worried about looking like a pussy— she can tell that I'm a bad boy. In fact, drinking wine makes me look even tougher, in my opinion. The way I look, most chicks would expect me to drink beer and whiskey, and I like to keep them guessing. "Jesus, this crazy long-haired rocker just ordered a wine, maybe I don't know what to expect in the bedroom." I drink it with my pinky sticking out, look across the table at the beautiful girl I'm dining with, and give her a little wink.

I would not, however, suggest drinking wine all night if you're out on the town (if we're going out after dinner, I'll switch to tequila). Also, I can't drink wine for more than a couple of hours because it makes me tired—especially red. And don't drink red wine at all if you're on a date . . . or out in public; it makes your teeth turn purple and it's very unattractive. Stick with the white, unless you're at home watching a movie or reading a book before bed.

TO LEAD A PEOPLE, YOU MUST WALK AMONG THEM

It's good for business for me to go out and party, even on nights that I'm not working. The more I go out and have fun with the kids, the more likely they are to start hanging out at my bar. I just have to make sure that I'm always the sexiest guy at the party, that I'm having a good time, and not *pretending* that I'm having a good time. If I'm faking it, I know I've been going out too much. If I feel like I've had one too many drinks to stay in control, or that I'm about to say stupid shit around people that respect me, I'll do the Irish dip. (I hate saying good-bye. Saying good-bye is like saying you're giving up on a party, or admitting that you're not having fun. I am having fun! I'm having a little too much fun, actually, and I need to get my ass to bed!) By the time I do the dip—usually around two A.M.— everyone is typically too drunk to notice anyway. And the earlier I dip out, the more time I have tomorrow to work out, or go for a run, or clean my room, or get something—anything— done. If I don't get shit done, I can't enjoy myself when I'm out partying. I have to have all my bills paid, my bed made, and 150 push-ups done before I can even *begin* to let loose and enjoy myself at a party.

Ask yourself this: Are women more likely to be attracted to a drunk, broke, flabby dude with a messy apartment, or to a slightly intoxicated guy who makes decent bucks, who has ripped arms and a flat stomach, and a clean apartment with fresh sheets for them to fuck on? Okay, actually, the truth of the matter is that I used to get *more* women when I was broke, flabby, and completely wasted all the time—but those women were sloppy twenty-two-year-olds, the kind of women who messed up my sheets and asked for cab fare in the morning. These women are known as cheeseburgers,* by the way, and

---

*Cheeseburger (chēz-bər-gər): N. Female.

  1. A sloppy, coked-up trash bag.

  2. A girl to be enjoyed on rare occasions, usually alongside a bunch of beers on a Sunday afternoon.

Oh, that girl is a cheeseburger. I took her ass home last week; she wanted to stay up until eight A.M. doing coke, and she didn't have enough money left to take the subway home in the morning.

they're to be enjoyed only once in a while, just like real cheeseburgers.

Now that I'm in shape, I only want to be with a quality woman, someone with a real job who smells nice and wears killer shoes. I want smoked salmon: expensive, healthy, and delicious. And since a nice piece of smoked salmon doesn't belong on a paper plate, I make sure my sink isn't full of dirty dishes. By the way, whatever happened to good old monogamous sex? Has the male species become so incredibly insecure that they have to sleep with as many partners as they possibly can, just so they can call their friends and basically admit what a douche bag they are? Whatever happened to chivalry and knights in shining armor? It takes an immature fuck to bang a bunch of drunk girls. It takes a real man to keep one girl happy for the rest of her life. Be a gentleman, you fuck.

THE NEW ME

On a Sunday night in October, I was covering a shift at the bar when a buddy of mine stopped in for a drink. "Fuck it, bro," I told him. "It's Sunday. Let's have some beers." I had two Red and White Dynamites. The first one I thoroughly enjoyed. The second was a little tougher to swallow. By the time I cracked open the third one, I was over it. The old me would have pounded beers all night, closed the bar, and walked across the street to an after-hours joint and partied 'til the sun came up. But the new healthy, sexy me was more interested in getting to bed and having a productive day. This was a turning point in my heavy drinking lifestyle. Now it's not uncommon for me to go a week without drinking.

I've done some calculations, and I figured out that it takes at least 500 calories to get me drunk. (Five hundred calories of wine translates to about one full bottle; 500 calories of whiskey would be about five shots; I need at least 750+ calories worth of beer, though, to feel anything.) The worst part is, that means I have to eat 500 fewer calories in food if I want to have the alcohol. Five hundred calories of beer, by the way, does not build muscle. On the other hand, 500 calories of grilled salmon and mixed greens does build muscle . . . and character, and self esteem. It's a never-ending battle that I struggle with daily; the booze or the mirror.

I think a lot of my desire to change my drinking habits also has to do with the fact that I'm getting older, and the older I get, the earlier I find myself going to bed. There's no way in hell I can stay out 'til five A.M. every night anymore. I just can't do it. Human beings are not nocturnal; it is not in our DNA to be up that late. The body wants to see as much sun as possible. These days, it's not uncommon for me to go to bed at midnight on nights that I'm not working. I suppose for a normal person midnight might seem pretty late, but for a party person it's unheard of. Of course, how much I work out is also a big factor. Sleep is incredibly important to the body when you're working out; it needs that time to rest and repair your muscles after all the heavy shit I put them through at the gym. So around midnight, my body is usually saying, "Hey, fucker, it's time for bed." The older I get, and the more I work out, the less I drink. But that's okay, because I'd rather be shredded than drunk.

PART II

IRON MAIDEN CHANGED MY LIFE
OR,
HOW NOT TO LOOK LIKE AN ASSHOLE
WHEN YOU'RE WORKING OUT

CHAPTER SIX

Don't Be a Meathead

LÜC'S LAW: IF YOU LIKE THE WAY SOMEONE LOOKS, ASK HIM
ABOUT HIS WORKOUT ROUTINE. DON'T BE SHY.

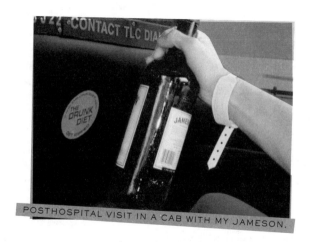

POSTHOSPITAL VISIT IN A CAB WITH MY JAMESON.

t was six P.M. on a Saturday, and I'd just gotten a text from
one of my bartenders, informing me that a squirrel had run
into St. Jerome's. Apparently, the little fucker had tried to
get out through the back, crashed into a mirror, and then ran
back out the front door. Several hours later I was at work, trying to sort out some problem with the DJ booth—DJ booth
problems are never-ending, by the way; DJs are the drunkest,
highest, most irresponsible people in the world—when my
door guy came over and whispered in my ear: "Hey, man, there's
a rat curled up in the corner."

You've got to be fucking kidding me, I thought. *When in the hell did my bar turn into a zoo?* I put the DJ booth situation on hold and went over to the corner of the bar with a flashlight, trying to be discreet so the customers wouldn't catch on. And what do I see? The squirrel that had wandered in for a beer earlier that afternoon. (He must have gotten a little too drunk to find his way out this time.) He also looked wounded, but he was still breathing and moving his head around when I shined the flashlight on him.

I spent a moment assessing the situation. Better to get this fucking squirrel out of my bar before two A.M., when he might suddenly feel well enough to start strutting around and freaking out all the ladies in their cocktail dresses. I grabbed a big black industrial trash bag and (quickly and quietly) wrapped it around the little guy and tried to pick him up. It turns out that wounded squirrels are a lot stronger than you might think—this little fucker must have been doing push-ups in the corner and eating red meat for the past three hours; he tried to furiously wiggle his way out of my grasp. Then he grabbed hold of the carpet in the DJ booth (I told you, it's just never-ending problems in there) and *would . . . not . . . let . . . go.* I knew that if he managed to get loose, there'd be a lot of women screaming at the top of their lungs, the bar would clear out in no time, and nobody would be making any money. (Also, someone would probably be calling the Health Department on my ass).

I squeezed tighter, trying to tear this rodent away from the carpet he was holding on to for dear life, and I somehow managed to rip him free, wrap him in the trash bag, and take one step for the door—and then the little fucker bit my finger! Hard enough to cut through the trash bag *and* my skin. It hurt like hell, but all I could think was, *I have to get this fucking squirrel out of here.* So I walked down the street and threw the fucker in a trash can. (For all you animal lovers out there, I live in New York; it's not like I was going to be able to gently release him into the wild, ok? Also, I seriously considered smacking that bag on the sidewalk a few times, after what he did to my finger.)

As I walked back to the bar, watching the blood drip from my finger, there was only one thought echoing in my mind: *Rabies.* But I had a bar full of people to worry about, so I washed my hands for five minutes straight in our world-famous, disgusting bathroom and got my ass back to work. When I finally had a second to breathe, I leaned over and asked a friend of mine to get on her phone and Google "rabies," to find out if I could survive five or six hours without getting a shot. She called her mother, who works at a hospital, and her mother informed her that there are no symptoms of rabies when contracted from a small rodent, and that in as little as ten hours the disease can spread to your vital organs and cause death.

Well, that's fucking great, that's exactly what I want to be thinking about while I'm busting my ass making drinks for hundreds of drunk assholes. I walked over to the DJ. "Listen," I told him, "if I pass out, I want you to run to the bar next door and get one of the bartenders to come fill in for me. Then I want you to get the door guy, and the two of you should throw me in the back of a cab, give the driver twenty bucks, and tell him to take me to the hospital on Twenty-sixth Street and First Avenue." I worked the rest of my shift, tried not to panic, and looked in the mirror every so often to make sure I wasn't foaming at the mouth.

When I closed the bar six hours later, I Googled "24-hour veterinarians" in Manhattan and called one and asked what I should do. (I figured if I called an actual hospital, no one would answer the phone, and I'd be stuck in one of those never-ending, automated hellholes of an answering service.) The vet told me to go to a human hospital *immediately*. And then he mentioned that it would be best to bring the squirrel with me.

Wait, *what*? Bring the fucking squirrel *with me*? Are you fucking serious? I called the human hospital to find out if that was really necessary. (If you hit zero, by the way, someone actually picks up.) Some woman answered, and I told her the whole story. "Oh, my God, let me get you a doctor," she said.

A few minutes later, the doctor got on. "You're going to need to come in immediately and get tetanus and rabies shots," she told me.

"So, uh, should I bring the squirrel with me?" I asked.

"Yes! Of course! We'll have to run some tests on it."

For Christ's sake. At this point, all the lights were on in the bar and all the customers were gone—which was a good thing—so I walked around the corner to see if I could find a trash bag with a dead squirrel in it. For some reason, the bag had migrated to the middle of the street—when I got within two feet of it, it moved! After hanging out in a trash bag for six hours, he was still alive! This was one tough fucking squirrel, I thought. I brought him back to the bar, wrapped two additional trash bags around him, and hailed a cab.

Considering that it was a Saturday night (or Sunday morning, technically), the hospital wasn't as busy as I'd expected—a few homeless people, a few sorry bastards who were too drunk to know where they were, and a crazy guy in handcuffs, with shackled feet and his very own police escort. He was obviously a mental patient—he kept screaming at everyone—and, lucky for me, I was instructed to sit next to him (it was a pretty small waiting room). I glared at him a few times, so he'd know that I was not okay with him talking, or even looking at me, and hoped it was enough to keep the psycho at bay. The squirrel, meanwhile, sat lifeless on the floor between my feet. I'd made his presence known, introduced him to everyone in the room (except the mental patient, of course), and informed everyone of the crazy chain of events. By that point, the little guy and I were on a first-name basis. I'd been calling him "Peter" for the last three hours.

Twenty minutes later, I got moved to another room filled with dirty, destitute people in beds, all hooked up to machines making loud beeping noises. (It wasn't the world's classiest hospital, but shit, I didn't have health insurance.) Eventually, the doctor that I'd spoken with on the phone came in and yelled out, "Where's the squirrel guy?"

"That's me!" I called out.

And do you know what she fucking told me? Squirrels don't carry rabies, after all.

Okay, I'll admit it: That story doesn't really have shit to do with dieting or exercise. Except that the entire time I was sitting in that waiting room, the only thing I could think about was how this damn squirrel was now fucking up my whole weekend. I mean, what kind of job requires a guy to get bit by vermin but doesn't give him benefits or health insurance? Now, not only was the situation costing me time, money, and sleep, it was costing me time with my running shoes. Even though I tried to distract myself by joking around with the homeless guys, I couldn't stop thinking about how I probably wouldn't be able to get a run in the next day if I actually had rabies.

I can't pinpoint the exact moment when running and working out became a huge part of my daily life, or when I began planning work around running, rather than the other way around. But looking back on it now, the drama with the squirrel was a real turning point in my quest to get sexy; it was the first time I can remember when being healthy was more important to me than having a good time. Of course, it wasn't always like that . . .

IN THE BEGINNING

For most of my life, I was always on the verge of having some kind of healthy workout routine. When I was a kid, for example—I must have been fourteen years old—my brother and I got a used all-in-one gym for Christmas. We bolted it to the wall in the basement and I would do leg curls, pull-downs, and the bench press. It was actually a nice little setup for a couple of teenagers. Fifteen years later, it's still in my parents' basement, collecting dust. (But only because—thank God— I don't actually live with my parents anymore.)

Growing up, I was actually fairly active and my father was always encouraging me to do lots of activities. I wouldn't exactly call myself an *athlete*, but I was usually doing something. My dad coached my soccer team (and my brother's, too), and I played baseball up until my last year of high school. But by the time I was a senior, I was more interested in playing drums than sports, so I quit. (He never let me live that down.) I just wasn't very good at it. Though, I later found out that my depth perception only functions at about 10 percent of normal, so maybe that's why I couldn't hit the damn ball.

As a freshman in college, I went back to hitting the gym pretty regularly. Of course, I had no idea what the fuck I was doing in there—I was the douche that goes for the heaviest weight on the rack because I didn't want anyone to think I was a pussy. I'd end up lifting the weight all wrong, which is completely counterproductive. Then I got thrown out of the dorms for having too many parties, so I moved into an apartment and stopped working out altogether.

Shortly after moving to New York, I decided to try again, and I went looking for a gym to join. At the time, I didn't even have a credit card, but the gym wouldn't accept cash. I had to open a bank account just to sign up! Then I had to make sure there was $69 in there on the seventeenth of every month. Jesus, this was a big responsibility. But I took the plunge; I signed up. And for the first six years of my membership, I was more concerned with being overdrawn on my account than I was with working out.

When I first decided to get sexy, I knew that I was finally going to have to get serious about working out. But I still didn't know what I was doing, so I would kind of half-ass it with the weight machines for thirty minutes or so, then I'd go downstairs and hit the elliptical machine for ten minutes, stretch, and call it a day. This, in combination with my new diet, actually worked for the first month; I had lost some weight for the first time in my life. But after a month of fucking around, I had reached that first plateau. The old me, as you know by now, would have just given up and gone back to sitting around on the couch watching *Seinfeld*, eating a frozen Snickers bar like a fat ass that never gets laid. Not that I had any desire to get laid back then; my sex life and self-esteem were both in the shitter. But the new me wasn't ready to give up.

It didn't take a fucking rocket scientist to figure out that I was going to need a new routine, a more effective way to work out—dicking around in the gym once or twice a week for the first few weeks may have helped me drop a few pounds, but it sure as hell wasn't going to get me looking like a prizefighter. So I bought a bunch of books and fitness DVDs—all of which were written and hosted by total meatheads who do nothing but lift weights all day—and a bunch of "health" magazines, which weren't much different. In fact, I quickly realized that the magazines would completely contradict themselves from month to month; one month it would say how X was the new miracle food, and that eating it would cure cancer, and the next month it would say that X contributes to belly fat and you should replace it with Y. That's about the time I stopped believing everything I read. After all, these fuckers will put anything on the cover of a magazine to get you to buy it. In desperation, I bought one of those hard-core muscle magazines, hoping to learn a little something about getting bigger, but I couldn't even flip through it—the thing had advertisements for "legal" steroids in the back, and the guys in the pictures were so huge and disgusting, I couldn't even look at them.

My goal has never been, nor will it ever be, to look like a fucking huge, ripped meathead. I always wanted to look something like Sean Connery as James Bond, or Paul Stanley or Bon Scott in '79, or Burt Reynolds in *Smokey and the Bandit*. It's just obvious that the guys with the huge, shaved, tan, steroid look are overcompensating for something; not necessarily having a small cock, although that's the first thing that comes to mind, but it could be any number of things. It could be that they wish they were taller, or that they wish they hadn't lost all their hair at twenty-six. The thing is, you don't have to lift weights seven days a week and eat nothing by whey powder to have great arms and nice abs, and you shouldn't overcompensate for your insecurities by becoming a Mr. Meathead. (Of course, that's easy for me to say—I'm 6'3" and I have a ridiculous head of hair.)

ASK STUPID QUESTIONS

I'm kind of shy with people I don't know—although you would never think that by looking at me—but I knew that if I wanted to figure out how to work my way around a gym without looking like an asshole, I was going to need some help. I wasn't getting it from books or magazines, so I started asking questions like an eight-year-old, grilling people like one of those annoying kids who never stops asking why the grass is green or the sky is blue. Anyone I met who looked good, or looked like they might work out, anyone who did yoga, played softball, or was wearing running shoes, I asked about their routine. A bit of advice: I've learned that when asking people questions about their workout habits, it's best to play dumb—pretend like you've never worked out before and you have absolutely no clue where to start. People are often very set in their ways when it comes to their fitness routine, and they're not interested in your fucking opinions. So it's best to keep you mouth shut; you just might learn something.

For instance, one of the security guys at St. Jerome's is a black belt in karate and capoeira, so I told him I was frustrated because I didn't really know what my end goals should be—exactly how much weight should I try to lose? How would I know if I was *really* looking better? With all my hard work, I didn't even know if I was getting good results. "Forget the scale," he told me. "I don't even own one. You have to take pictures of yourself with no clothes on from time to time and compare them."

Shit, what a great idea! The next day I stripped down to my purple tight-whiteys, put my camera on top of the stereo, and set the timer for ten seconds. From then on, I took a new photo every month to document my progress, and I kept all the pictures in a folder on my desktop called "weight loss," so that I could compare them, side by side. This helped tremendously, and it's just one of the many instances where I learned something by asking a stupid question.

Here's another one: I had read somewhere that, to be

more productive in the gym, you should do more repetitions with smaller weights, so I had started off doing three sets of fifteen reps on four different machines. One day I'd work my triceps and chest, the next day I'd work my biceps and back. I'd throw in some leg shit here and there, too, just because I thought I was supposed to, even though I didn't really care about having muscular legs. Who looks at a dude's legs, anyway? But then I talked to this friend of mine who is totally ripped (he's been working out his whole life) and described my routine to him, and he suggested that I increase from three sets of fifteen to four sets of ten. Genius! Even though I wasn't excited about doing more sets, I was excited to see results. (Generally speaking, sets with fewer reps help build the muscles' strength and size, while sets with many reps—like, fifteen or more—are better for increasing endurance.)

I asked another one of my regulars—this totally jacked guy who always wears white T-shirts to show off his muscles—what kind of weight machines he used. "All free weights, dumbbells, and barbells," he told me. "No machines." What an interesting concept. I had never even touched a dumbbell before; I had always walked right past them in the gym (kind of like how I had always walked past all the fresh produce in the grocery store on my way to the frozen food section). This guy also taught me that a curl will make the biceps grow upward, but that if you turn your wrist 90 degrees (so that your thumb faces the sky and your pinky finger faces the ground), and do what's called a hammer curl, the biceps will grow wider. I was amazed, and I couldn't wait to try it. And after just one week doing hammer curls, I noticed my biceps getting wider. I shit you not. The very next time I saw that guy I bought him a beer.

Eventually, I convinced myself to talk to the lady behind the counter at the gym, Linda—who, it turned out, was more than happy to answer all my questions. She liked helping me along on my journey to become the sexiest man on Earth. I'd tell her my problem of the day, and she'd give me a few suggestions to fix it. She'd even train me every now and then, if the place was empty and she didn't have anything else to do. (I go to a small, noncorporate gym in my quiet little neighborhood, and I go at odd times because I work odd hours; it's almost always empty.) I even started taking classes—I signed up for a one-day-a-week spin class, since Linda was the instructor. Yes, it sounds totally stupid, but I was in there with some smoking hot chicks, and they inspired me to push myself harder. I figured if a bunch of chicks can do this shit, then I'd better be busting my ass. (They also gave me something nice to look at while I was sweating my balls off.)

After a month of spin classes, I was so into cycling that I decided to buy myself a decent bicycle. Even some of my friends were getting into bikes, although they were into fixed-gear track bikes, the favored mode of transportation for smelly bearded guys from Brooklyn. I am more of a purist. I mean, I was going to be riding on a road, so I figured I should get myself a road bike, right? Plus, a road bike has brakes, whereas a track bike does not. I'm not a fucking idiot. In a town full of potholes and assholes driving cabs, I wanted some good goddamn brakes so I could keep myself out of accidents and avoid any reconstructive surgery on my pretty face.

Perhaps in some towns it's considered pussy to ride a bike around. You may look like a total nerd and get a lot of laughs around the office for showing up with a helmet under your arm, forty-year-old-virgin style. But riding a bike in New York City is easily the most dangerous form of transportation, rendering any accusations about testicle size null and void. So I asked a friend of mine who had the coolest, most expensive bike in my whole crew to take me to a bike shop. He used to be a bike messenger in Philadelphia, so I assumed he would know a thing or two about what kind of bike to get, or at least where to buy one. He took me to a place just a few blocks from my bar and, sure enough, he was friends with half the guys that worked there. Having not purchased a bike for myself since I was eleven (using my paper route money), I was a little embarrassed to walk into a bicycle store as a grown-ass man. But after just a few minutes, it was made very clear to me that if you want to be a cyclist in this city, you must have balls of steel. A test of my manhood was exactly what I was looking for at that point in my life, so I bought myself a $700 road bike. (I had to borrow $100 from my buddy to cover the total cost, but it was worth every fucking penny.) I named her Delilah and, for a while there, we were inseparable. I rode her everywhere—to the movies, to the supermarket, to work. (It only took me twenty minutes to ride my bike to work, whereas the subway takes a half hour. Though I wasn't so concerned with saving time, it was more about burning the calories.)

When you find some new hobby that you really enjoy—be it stamp collecting, racecar driving, bowling, or oral sex—it's only natural that you'll want to get better at it. (And if you become *really* fucking good at something, you might even get paid to do it, and that's when you've found yourself what's known as a career.) Right up until the time that I decided to get sexy, I'd been better at partying than anything else. But even this asshole knew that you can't party for a living forever—when you're fifty years old and still working in the professional party world, "retirement" usually means "rehab." By the third month of my new life, I was hitting the gym no less than three times a week and riding Delilah to work as often as possible, and the more time I spent working out, the more I actually started to *like* working out. I knew that if I kept it up, I'd be sexy by summer, just in time to strut my shit on the beach for the first time in my life. Practice makes perfect, as they say, and I was really enjoying the practice. I was practicing to have a better body. I was practicing to be happy.

What the fuck is a Track Bike?
Track Bike: A bicycle that was designed specifically for riding on a track

So, a track bike only has one gear, which is fixed to the back wheel. That means, if the wheel is moving the pedals are moving. Also, it has no brakes. The only way to stop a track bike is to apply reverse pressure to the pedals with your feet until you slow down to a stop. You see, they are meant to be ridden on a track, going in a circle, at a high rate of speed. There are no stop signs on a track. No stop lights, no traffic, no children, no pedestrians, no potholes, and no fucking cab drivers. For whatever reason, the hipsters of Brooklyn have adopted the track bike as their own. The only reasons I can come up with for this are that (A) track bikes are difficult to ride unless you're actually on a track, and (B) they're therefore dangerous, making them an incredibly stupid choice for anyone living in a densely populated urban environment. Hipsters, however, tend to make lots of stupid decisions, like listening to crappy emo music. So maybe the track bike makes sense for them after all.

I'm going to fast-forward for a minute here and tell you a story. About a year after I bought Delilah, I signed up for a 300-mile bike ride from Boston to New York City to raise money for the LGBT Center on Thirteenth Street in Manhattan. Yes, 300 miles—100 miles a day for three straight days. Honestly, I had no clue what I was getting myself into. I saw a sign at the diner in my neighborhood about the ride and

MY FIRST THREE-HUNDRED-MILE BIKE RIDE.

said, "Fuck it, I would love to be able to tell the world that I rode my bike from Boston to New York." (It was another test of my manhood, just what I was looking for.)

After signing up, I went to a training session at the Center. I still had eight months before the big ride, and at that point I had been working out for over a year and was fairly confident with the shape I was in . . . but *300 fucking miles?* What the hell was I thinking? Was I really going to be ready for this thing? I went out and bought myself an even better bike; I custom ordered a brand-new top-of-the-line Trek. It even had my name on it. I figured if I was going to do a serious ride, I'd better have a serious fucking bike. I put a down payment on it, and a few weeks later my new bike came in. I was so broke at the time that I borrowed the money from petty cash at my bar. Don't worry, though, I put it back a few days later, after picking up some extra shifts. That's just the point, though: If you want something—if you truly want something bad enough—you'll get it. And I wanted to ride my bike from Boston to New York. The fact that it was for a good cause was just icing on the cake.

I took my brand-new fancy bike with the clips and the pedals and my new spandex butt-pad shorts and went out for my first really long ride. I started in Brooklyn, rode to the George Washington Bridge, into Jersey, and headed north until the sun went down. Then I turned around and came back, and tried not to get lost. Altogether, I made it fifty-six miles. Still, all I could think was, how the fuck am I going to ride 100 miles per day for three fucking days? I did it, though. In fact, I kicked ass.

There were a number of pretty fucking serious riders at the event. One guy had even done some Ironman triathlons, so I followed him around like he was some kind of God and tried to sit as close to him as possible during lunch breaks. I'd already signed up for my first marathon, just two and a half months away. (I was signing up for anything and everything I could get my hands on.) I asked him how a marathon was going to compare to the bike ride, and he told me I'd have no problem. I didn't believe him.

On the second day of the race, he asked me to join his paceline. I didn't even know what a paceline was, but it seemed like a cool invitation. (For you all noncyclers: A paceline is kind of like a big game of Follow the Leader—the riders in your group cycle one behind the other in a single-file line; the guy out front is actually working the hardest, because he's got the most wind resistance to deal with. He provides a shelter from the wind, allowing the other riders to draft. When he gets tired, he moves to the left and falls to the end of the paceline, and the next rider in the line takes his place.)

When it was my turn to be out in front, I gave it everything I had. I didn't want these guys to think I couldn't handle it, so I pushed as hard and as fast as I could. Immediately, the Ironman guy dropped out of the paceline—he said he couldn't keep up with my ass! (Technically, the guy at the front isn't supposed to increase speed, but I didn't want to disappoint anybody.) And the points is: I wore out a guy who's done Ironmans. Yes, he was twenty-five years older than me, but that's not the fucking point. The point is that I surprised even myself; and you can, too.

YOU DON'T NEED FANCY EQUIPMENT

Let's face it; gyms are intimidating. Just setting foot in one, even before you've actually signed up for a membership, is a huge accomplishment. And back when I first considered joining a gym, I was scared shitless. I thought there would be jacked-up, sweaty, tan guys all over the place, looking at me like I was a loser. I had no idea what to wear. I didn't know what to do with my hair; should I pull it up or let it hang out?

The truth is, gyms are filled with people exactly like you. No matter how fit they are, they still worry about what you think when you look at them, *especially* the huge meathead-types, those *JACKED* magazine-reading, steroid-using idiots. But the good news is, you don't actually need a bunch of fancy machines, or even a gym membership, to get shredded. All you need is a floor and some sort of bar to pull yourself up on, whether that's a $30 pull-up bar you buy from the sports-supply store, or the scaffolding outside your apartment. If you focus, push yourself to the limit, and pay attention to form, doing push-ups and pull-ups is really all you need to get an amazing body. Why? Because push-ups and pull-ups use your own body weight as resistance. (Any idiot can pick up a fifteen-pound dumbbell and curl it twenty times, but you've got to be in pretty good shape to heft your fat 250-pound ass off the floor.) Throw in a little core work once or twice a week, and you're set for life. Of course, that doesn't mean you can fuck around doing just ten push-ups a day and have the world's greatest beach body, unless that sort of thing runs in your family.

Push-Ups

I was shooting the shit with Georgie one afternoon—you remember him, he's the guy in charge of the Motherfucker, the badass Rock 'N' Roll party in New York—when push-ups came up in the conversation. I asked him how many he could do. "Sixty," he said, and I nearly shit myself. I was only doing twenty to twenty-five, and at that point, I had already been lifting weights for a couple of months. Well, that was it. Lüc Carl doesn't let anyone do anything better than him. So I started doing push-ups just about every day. Before I knew it, I was up to forty . . . then forty-five . . . then fifty.

A month or so later, I had a friend over for Sunday Funday, and we randomly started doing push-ups. We'd had a few beers, so our egos had kicked in, and we decided to take turns to see who could do more. He went first, and I noticed that he was doing them a lot better than I was. My lazy ass wasn't going near as close to the floor, and I'd been going about twice as fast. Fuck! I tried them his way and I could only do twenty. Here I thought I had been kicking ass; little did I know my forty-five shitty push-ups were the equivalent of twenty real push-ups. I was back to square one (and pissed about it).

What the fuck is *Circuit Training?*
Circuit training: A form of conditioning combining resistance training and high-intensity aerobics

Basically, circuit training means you're moving from one exercise to another without stopping to rest in between; a typical circuit consists of three different exercises, but you could include anywhere from two to 100. (Circuit training is also a great way to bust through a plateau in your weight loss and get those muscles really looking good in the mirror.)

To get your heart pumping and the sweat flowing, try this: do a set of ten to twelve biceps curls with your right hand, then with your left hand, then drop down and do fifteen push-ups; perform all three exercises right in row without stopping. (So all three sets become one big set.) Rest for thirty to sixty seconds after the push-ups, and then do it all over again a total of three or four times. If you've done the whole rotation three or four times and you're not feeling like you're going to die, do it again! What have you got to lose?

I gave up on push-ups for a few weeks after that. Fuck you, push-ups. That was my attitude. Eventually, however, I came back to my senses and tried again. I started off by doing at least twenty at a time, and it was really kicking my ass. Then I decided that rather than shoot for twenty-two to twenty-five, which wasn't working, I'd spread them out—I'd do twenty, wait an hour or so, and then see if could do twenty more. If I could only do fifteen or so on the second time around, that was okay. "We're finally getting somewhere," I said to myself. "That makes it thirty-five push-ups for the day; not bad, fucker."

I started doing twenty at a time—attempting a new set every few hours—until I couldn't do any more. Now I'm to the point where I can do at least 100 per day, every other day; 200 is a great day. Sometimes I drop down and do twenty or thirty push-ups during my one-minute rest between sets at the gym.

Push-ups are now one of my favorite things in the world, right up there with beer; they're just the best thing out there when it comes to getting kick-ass arms. There are dozens of

variations—try them with your hands close together, with your hands far apart, or with just one arm—so you can isolate a particular section of your chest or triceps. Plus, you can do them anywhere, anytime; it doesn't even matter what you're wearing. Sure, you might look like a jackass if you drop down and crank out thirty while you're making copies at work, but as long as your boss doesn't mind, fuck it. Hell, sometimes if it's early on a Saturday night, I'll ask the DJ to put on "Eye of the Tiger" and I'll drop down and do push-ups right there in the fucking bar. Every other guy in the place always ends up dropping down and trying to do more than me and, of course, they never can. They'll do fifteen or twenty half-assed, too-fast push-ups, then go back to their beer and tell me about how many they used to do when they were a wrestler in high school. Well, guess what? I couldn't even do *one* push-up in high school. But I can do a fuckload more push-ups than you now. (And while you're pouting, I'll be on the other side of the bar with the hot girls. You're not welcome over here, ass-hole.)

Here's some advice: Drop down to the floor, right now, and see how many push-ups you can do (and we're talking about real push-ups here; chest to the ground, no bullshit). The average male should be able to do at least ten push-ups, even if he doesn't work out. For women, the number is around three. If you can't even do one, try them from your knees. And don't forget to breathe! Breathe in on your way up and out on your way down. When your arms are shaking and you can't force yourself to do even one more, stop and breathe deep. Feel the burn in your arms and chest. Learn to love that burn. One hour later, drop down and try again. Add up how many you did throughout the day, write that number down on your calendar, and be proud of your progress. Even if you started out doing ten, you'll be up to twelve in a few days, and up to twenty in a week or so. Push yourself to the limit every time.

Pull-Ups and Chin-Ups

My buddy Johnny used to have a chin-up bar in his apartment. One night, years ago, I was over there drinking some beers and shooting pool when he started doing chin-ups. He did twelve. So, of course, I went over there and gave it a shot. I couldn't even do one. Once again, my ego kicked in—this

is a guy who once had a mirror cut to fit his kitchen table, which always had a mound of coke piled on it, right underneath the Mötley Crüe poster on his wall. I didn't think he should be able to do *anything* better than me, so I immediately went out and bought myself a chin-up bar. I tried once or twice more, and couldn't even get myself off the ground, so I threw it in the closet and forgot about it for months. Fuck you too, chin-up bar.

Eventually, I decided to give chin-ups a try again, but not without some help. There's a pull-up assist machine at my gym; it's like doing regular pull-ups, only the weights on the machine counteract the weight of your body, decreasing the amount of weight you're actually lifting. (For example, if you weigh 200 pounds and you set the machine for fifty pounds, you'll only be lifting 150 pounds.) Basically, the machine makes pull-ups easier. I used that machine for at least a few months before attempting to do another real, honest-to-God pull-up by myself. Even after all that practice, I still couldn't even do one! I could, however, manage six chin-ups. (Chin-ups, by the way, are done with your palms facing you. Pull-ups, on the other hand, are done with your palms facing away from you; they mainly work the upper back. Since there are more muscles involved in a chin-up than a pull-up, they're a bit easier—you're pulling yourself up with more than one, specific muscle group.)

These days, pull-ups are still the most difficult part of all my exercise routines. I have an entire workout that is nothing but different types of pull-ups and chin-ups. I'll max myself out on every damn chin-up bar in the gym over the course of forty-five minutes until my palms hurt so much I can't even open a door.

Start out small, in the privacy of your own home. If you can't even do one, pull up a chair and rest your feet on it—that'll make them a bit easier. Once you can do two or three, you can graduate to trying at the gym (you know, in front of other people), as well as experimenting with different grips.

Here are some examples of pull-ups and chin-ups I include in my routine:

- Alternate grips; one hand, palm facing your body, the other hand, palm facing away
- Change the width of your grip; do a few reps with your hands close together, and a few reps with your hands spaced far apart
- Pull your knees to your chest while doing pull-ups

What the fuck is Maxing Out?
Maxing out: Reaching the full extent or allowance

Maxing out simply means you've worked yourself to the point where you can't work yourself anymore. And I'm not talking about packing boxes in a factory to the point where you can't pack one more box because you want to get home to that six-pack of Budweiser. I'm talking about curling a dumbbell until you physically can't fucking curl it anymore. While it's great to work out your muscles to the point of exhaustion, maxing out does *not* mean you should reach for the heaviest weight, lift it once, and wind up breaking your arm in the process. Don't be a dumbass.

Abdominals

You know what I find strange? In the last five years or so, it's become completely acceptable—preferable even—for a woman to be a little bit thick, to have some junk in the trunk. At the same time, however, men are almost *expected* to have a washboard stomach. I blame this on the rise of hip-hop. The guys in those videos are all absolutely shredded, yet they're singing about big fat asses. Not that there's a problem with that, I love a big fat ass as much as I love a shot of whiskey and a beer. But what I want to know is, how did we manage to make a big dump truck ass sexy (see also: meatball*), while—at the very same time—creating a double standard that a man has to be totally ripped? Why does a man have to spend his days on the floor doing crunches while his woman can lie around eating cornbread? (I suppose, after all the years that women have been starved, tortured and forced to be thin by the media and society, this is fair. But fuck.) You know what else? Even though nearly all of the most recent studies on eating disorders have been aimed at women, the "experts" keep saying the same things about men: "Studies have shown that the incidence of eating disorders in men are increasing." I'm telling you, it's because of those damn videos! In fact, there should be a movement to change the name of abs to Hip-Hops.

Okay, fine, so the world is obsessed with abs, including you. Well, in order to understand how to get a six-pack, you've got to understand what the core muscles, our abs, were designed to do. These muscles are supposed to support the back, to keep the spine aligned and erect at all times, and to reduce the risk of back injury. If you think about it scientifically, without abs we'd all be walking around at 90-degree angles. So here's another question: How in the world did the sit-up become known as the universal exercise for Hip-Hops, when the primary move-

---

*Meatball (meet-bawl): N. Female.
   1. A deliciously thick girl with a big, fat, gorgeous ass. Generally has large tits and a small- to medium-sized midsection.
   2. A *cheeseburger* that is not a *dump truck*.
"Oh, my God, did you see the size of the ass on that meatball at the bar?"

ment of this exercise involves curling the spine into a position it isn't meant to be in?

Look, when you have a big fat beer gut like I did, sit-ups are completely counterproductive; unless you have very low body fat, they only make you look fatter. If you think about it, the abdomen is structured in such a way that the majority of the muscle is underneath the fat. So when you build up that muscle, you're pushing the fat out, too. I can remember when I first started doing sit-ups; I'd look in the mirror the next day and look worse than I had the day before. Then I'd want to kill myself. Why bother doing all that crap if it's going to make you look like you just ate two cheeseburgers? Like push-ups and pull-ups, I gave up on sit-ups (and core work altogether) for nearly three months.

In case you're wondering, yes, sit-ups *will* burn a little bit of fat, and if you do 500 sit-ups a day and eat right, you will have killer abs. But let's get real, most of us aren't motivated enough to do that every single day. Even when I got my body fat down to a respectable level, I discovered that sit-ups still weren't the most effective way to get great abs. These days, I hardly ever do traditional sit-ups, and when I do them, it's always on an incline, just like Mr. T from *Rocky III*. (If you do sit-ups on an incline bench or a Swiss ball, you'll have a greater range of motion, since you can crunch forward and extend backward. Crunches done on the floor, however, are only targeting one section of the abdomen, and they're not as effective.)

If you want to get ripped, you'll need a range of exercises to target the five major sets of muscles that make up your core. Get out your highlighter: I'm going to explain them here, and give you the best exercise for each group.

Muscle 1: Transverse Abdominis, also known as the "spare tire." This muscle acts like a belt, it wraps around your spine to give it support.

EXERCISE: THE PLANK

Get on your hands and knees (stop fucking laughing), palms flat on the floor, as if you were preparing to do a push-up. Now, kick your legs out straight so that you're balancing on your toes—again, just like a push-up—and then bend your arms and slowly lower your chest until it's about four or fives inches off the ground, keeping your body in a straight line by flexing your Hip-Hops. Hold the pose for sixty seconds, and

repeat three times (or until you reach exhaustion). If this particular pose is too difficult, try resting on your forearms—just make sure to keep your legs and midsection off the ground.

Once you become strong enough you can perform more difficult variations, like lifting one foot at a time and holding for sixty seconds, or balancing both feet up on a Swiss ball and holding for sixty seconds.

What the fuck is a *Swiss Ball*?
Swiss ball: A large, heavy-duty inflatable ball

Swiss balls, which are sometimes called exercise balls, stability balls, balance balls, or yoga balls (but never blue balls), are those big squishy balls you sometimes see people balancing on while doing crunches or core work at the gym; they were originally used back in the 1960s by Swiss physical therapists (meaning from Switzerland, you asshole) and chiropractors (hence the name). Swiss balls are great for improving core strength and coordination, since it takes a lot of effort to balance on one, as well as for targeting the abs when you're doing crunches. Just about every gym has some; if you're not sure what you're doing, don't be afraid to ask someone!

Muscle 2: External Oblique. You know those lines on either side of a ripped stomach, the ones that are basically like two big arrows pointing down to a dude's cock? The big muscles on the outside of that line are called the obliques; there are two of them, one on either side of the body. They make up the outer edge of the core and create that cut look.

EXERCISE: RUSSIAN TWIST

Get yourself into a crunch position; lie on your back, knees bent, feet flat on the ground. Now, while holding a single dumbbell with both hands, flex your midsection and hold the crunch. Then, twist your upper body from left to right. Aim for twenty-five reps.

The first time you try the Russian Twist, you should start out with a light weight—like a five-pounder—to make sure you're doing it correctly. Next time, reach for a heavier weight

RUSSIAN TWIST.

and shoot for ten reps. On your third try, use a twenty-pound weight and see how many reps you can crank out.

Muscle 3: Internal Oblique. These muscles lie underneath the external obliques, running in the opposite direction.

EXERCISE: CROSSOVER CRUNCH

Get yourself into a crunch position again, but instead of keeping both feet on the ground, cross your right leg over your left, so that your right ankle rests on top of your left knee. Start by aiming for twenty-five to fifty reps, gradually working up to 100 or so. Eventually, you want to perform this move to exhaustion (so, until you can't fucking do any more).

Muscle 4: Rectus Abdominis. This is where the term "abs" comes from; the abdominals are the long muscles that run down the

CROSSOVER CRUNCH.

front of your belly. These are the muscles that give you that six-pack look, but only if you have very low body fat. Once you drop a few pounds, you can start adding these exercises into your routine.

EXERCISE: Basic sit-ups and crunches are the most popular exercises to target the abdominal muscles, and there are literally hundreds of variations. Pick one.

Muscle 5: Erector Spinae. This is a group of three muscles that make up the back side of your core.

EXERCISE: BACK EXTENSIONS. Lie flat on your stomach, interlacing your fingers behind your head. Slowly raise your upper body and your legs at the same time, as if you were Superman flying through the air. Flex your Hip-Hops and back, keeping your toes and your chin as high as possible. Hold until exhaustion, and repeat.

BACK EXTENSIONS.

By the way, these are only a few examples of the literally hundreds of core exercises to choose from. Don't do the same exercise for more than four weeks in a row. Switch it up!

CHAPTER SEVEN

Running Is Like an Unattractive Woman

LÜC'S LAW: BUY NEW SHOES.

In the summer, I spend a decent amount of time fishing at this nice little pier on the western coast of Brooklyn, not far from the Statue of Liberty. It's beautiful down there, and I love being outside. In fact, I love being outside so much that I decided to try running outside, just for the hell of it. (I'd already been running a bit on the elliptical in the gym, so it seemed like the next natural step to take, anyway.) I didn't have the slightest clue how to get to my fishing spot on foot, but I knew the general direction. So one night in late February, about two months into my new routine, I put on my old basketball pants that I'd gotten for Christmas about eight years earlier, and laced up the gym shoes that I'd owned for three years—which still looked brand-new—and off I went.

I'm not even really sure what gave me the spark of motivation that first time. Whether it was being around my skinny, good-looking friends, or the fact that I still had plenty of time before T-shirt weather, I can't be sure. I was just ready. I didn't want to be fat and insecure anymore. I knew there was an incredibly sexy fucker under all that flab, and I was ready to meet him.

The pier is about 1.2 miles away from my apartment, each

way, and I told myself that it was okay to walk as much as I needed to. "Just get your ass down there and back, no matter how long it takes." I'd pulled my hair back, put on a hooded sweatshirt (it was already nine P.M. and only about 40 degrees out), and started blasting Metallica in my headphones. The whole time I was yelling at myself, "Don't stop, you fat fuck. You can do this . . . just one block at a time . . . keep going . . . never quit." When I finally got down to the pier and looked out at Lady Liberty, I felt like Rocky when he reaches the top of the stairs and throws his hands in the air. I stood there, soaking it all in for a minute, before turning and walking back down the pier toward home. When I got back to the street, I started running again.

Round-trip, it took a little over half an hour, which works out to around a thirteen-minute mile, which I was damn proud of for my first time. (I was more than willing to cut my fat ass a little slack.) And when I got back to my house, dripping in sweat, already feeling like a new man, I was so excited that I downloaded "Eye of the Tiger." Somehow, even after a miserable 2.4 miles (that I sort of hated every second of), I was already looking forward to my next run.

A few days later, I was back out there again, and this time I had "Eye of the Tiger" locked and loaded on my iPod. The song is just under five minutes long, and my goal was to try and make it down to the pier and back by the time the song had played through five times (so twenty-five minutes total). It really pumped me up, actually, and I wanted to keep pushing, to keep running the whole time without stopping to walk. I didn't make it, though. I wasn't ready. I was still chain-smoking cigarettes, for Christ's sake. And, of course, I was just incredibly out of shape in general; most of the time I felt like I was going to pass out. Still, it felt great to be doing something good for my body for a change, something that none of my sexy friends were out there doing.

I started setting goals and guidelines for myself to stay motivated. I made myself get going by four P.M. If it was 4:01 and I was still lacing up my shoes, I started to feel guilty (and that guilt was a good thing). If it was 40 degrees or warmer, I would run outside. If it was below 40, I'd go to the gym and work out on the elliptical machine or the treadmill. But for those first few months, I mostly felt like I was just forcing myself to do something that I didn't really want to do. I'd think of absolutely anything besides the fact that I was out there running, usually it was about the song that was blasting in my ears, or about what I was going to eat when I got home.

In the beginning, I think, I mainly started running because I was depressed. As I've already mentioned, my girlfriend had left me a few months earlier, and I had dug myself into a hole so deep that, no matter how little I ate or how hard I worked, I couldn't get out of it. I was fat and miserable, but her career was blossoming. I couldn't even watch reruns of *Seinfeld* without seeing her singing in her underwear during the fucking commercial breaks. I couldn't even drink the pain away in my own home—like a normal guy—because there she was, taking over the whole world right in front of my face. Even if I was just trying to buy beer, I'd have to listen to her sing about how great life is on the radio at the goddamn grocery store. If I went to the gym, she'd be on the TV doing a talk show or receiving an award for Most Amazing Person Ever. I was happy for her, of course, but I didn't really need my ex shoved down my throat. I basically had no choice but to run. And run is what I did. I bought a new pair of running shoes, threw away my remote control and logged off the Internet. The only way to escape was to get outdoors and run. The more I ran, the better I felt about myself, and the closer I got to being the person I wanted to be.

TACKLING SUICIDE HILL

Eventually, the weather got better and my "Rocky run" got boring. I'd always known that one day I would run in the other direction, down to the foot of the Brooklyn Bridge, about two and a half miles from my house, and that day had come. I remember how mild the weather was, and that I was wearing an AC/DC T-shirt, and that I just kept pushing myself. "Don't stop, you pussy. Just two more songs. Keep going."

Aside from fantasizing about the food I was going to eat when I got home, in the beginning of my running career I also found it helpful to look for milestones along the way, to break up the monotony. That first day that I ran to the foot of the bridge, I noticed a bunch of old mooring posts in the East River, poking up around the dock. I set my sights on one, and ran up and touched it. It's been my marker ever since.

I slowed down a bit to soak in the view of lower Manhattan and to catch my breath, and then I noticed a nearby gas station with a bunch of kick-ass old cars parked out front. With my hands on my head, still breathing heavy, I walked over. As I circled the back of a '55 Chevy, I noticed that the street next to the gas station ascended into a giant hill, and I was ready for it. "I'm Lüc Carl," I said to myself. "Fuck this hill." I took it on full steam.

The hill is only about three or four blocks long, but it's incredibly steep. By the time I got to the top, I couldn't breathe, I couldn't run, I couldn't even walk—but it didn't matter. I had taken that hill for all it was worth. I spent a few moments recovering, and then I started walking. I walked a lot during my runs back then. I'd jog as far as I could without feeling like

I was going to pass out, and then I'd walk for a while; it could have been five blocks or two miles—every run was different. (My lungs often couldn't keep up with my legs). But whenever I started walking, I'd always press pause on my iPod, so I wouldn't waste a high-energy song on the lazy part of my run. I didn't deserve to listen to the good stuff when I wasn't actually running. And when I'd caught my breath, I'd hit play and bask in the glory of metal.

I continued walking for a ways after the hill. I had no idea where the streets were taking me, but I knew I was headed back in the direction of my house. Then I found myself on a walking path that soars above the Brooklyn-Queens Expressway and overlooks lower Manhattan. It's called the Promenade, and while I had heard of it, I can't believe I'd never been there before. It's beautiful, and it's full of benches and flowers and shit-tons of people, including other runners. Personally, I find it very motivating to run when there are other people around; it pushes me even harder, and I usually end up picking up the pace quite a bit. Lots of people, however, have told me they feel uncomfortable running in places with lots of people around—yeah, because when you stop to walk, you feel like a pussy. Take it from me, find areas where there are tons of people and it will push you to become that much better.

After my kick-ass run—the farthest I had ever been—I was so fucking pumped that I wanted to call everyone I knew. I called my mother and told her that I'd just run five miles (she thought I was crazy, and kept offering to send me boxes of Oreos). The next time I went to the gym, I was so proud of myself that I told Linda all about it. She told me that the hill I had conquered actually has a name: Suicide Hill. *Jesus*, I thought, *someone who works at a gym calls it Suicide Hill, and I took it on? This drunk, chain-smoking fuck who ate French fries every day for fifteen years conquered* Suicide Hill?! *At' a boy!*

What the fuck is *Cardio*?
Cardiovascular: Of or pertaining to the heart and blood vessels

"Cardio" is short for cardiovascular, and any time you hear the term it means you're working out your heart. In case you're a total moron (and if you are, that's okay; I used to be one, too), a cardio exercise is anything that's going to make your heart beat faster than normal. Cardio not only burns calories, it helps you prevent shit like high blood pressure, high cholesterol, heart attacks, and diabetes.

Although getting a blow job would technically count as cardio, running is a better alternative when you're trying to lose weight. If you're not into running, you could try bicycling, jumping jacks, or—if you don't care what the neighbors think—there's always Rollerblading.

FUCK YOU, BRIDGE

I was out on one of my regular runs one day (I was probably putting in ten to twelve miles a week at that point), when I ran into this kid I used to play softball with—he'd also worked with me at the dive bar a few years back. He, like most people in my life, couldn't believe that I'd started running, and he commented on how good I looked, which felt amazing. I see most of my friends on a daily or weekly basis, so they weren't really noticing my weight loss. (When you see a person every single day, a weekly one- or two-pound weight loss isn't always obvious.) So this kid from the softball team mentioned that he used to run quite a bit before his wedding, but that he hadn't since. It had always been his goal, he told me, to run over the bridge, but he'd never made it. At that exact moment, running the bridge became my new goal; it was like something in my brain just clicked. I mean, I'd made it to the foot of the bridge and all, but it had never occurred to me to run *over* it. What a crazy idea. I knew I wasn't quite ready for the bridge *yet*, but I wanted to do it, just once, just to say that I did it. I wanted to be better than the softball kid. What the fuck, I want to better than everyone, at everything.

On a random Monday afternoon, after a few more weeks of running around the neighborhood, I finally felt ready. Every Monday I go into work early so I can take care of bar business for the week. So I just woke up, strapped on my running shoes, and said to myself, "Today's the day. Fuck that bridge." Seriously, I just decided to do it. You can't sit around waiting for an engraved invitation to shit like that, you just have to man up and go.

I picked the Manhattan Bridge, because the exit ramp is much closer to St. Jerome's than the exit ramp of the Brooklyn Bridge, and I knew that the shorter the distance I had to run in Manhattan, the better—it's a pain in the ass. (You know—people, cars, garbage, all that crap). What I didn't know is that the Manhattan Bridge is very long and very steep, and the only people walking over it are crackheads and weirdos— as opposed to the Brooklyn Bridge, which has a beautiful bike path and is always packed with tourists and pedestrians. I also managed to get lost on my way to the entrance ramp, so I stopped to ask a cop for directions. (I ended up going an extra half-mile out of my way before I even got there.) Once I reached the foot of the bridge, I looked up at that massive thing and said, "You are nothing. You were built by men; I am a man. I am better than you. I am going to kick your fucking ass."

Walking, I decided, was not going to be an option; I was going to run nonstop all the way to the other side (just shy of a mile-and-a-half away). I climbed the ten or so steps and didn't stop, looking for milestones the whole time. The Manhattan Bridge, which spans from a Brooklyn neighborhood called DUMBO—short for "Down Under the Manhattan Bridge Overpass"—to Canal Street in Manhattan (the Chinatown street where you can buy a whole bunch of fake designer shit for ten dollars) is made distinct by two blue arches; each one is about a third of the way from either end. I kept staring at that first arch and then back down at my feet, because I knew that the next time I looked up, I'd be closer. I kept pushing, kept yelling at myself while Iron Maiden pumped from my headphones. My legs were burning and my lungs were begging me to stop, but once I got to that first arch I just kept saying, "You're a third of the way there, man. Be proud. Only a pussy would stop now." Eventually I got to the point where I wasn't actually running uphill anymore, and I knew that meant I was halfway. I don't know if I've ever been more proud of myself. I was accomplishing some pretty kick-ass things for a kid from the cornfields of Nebraska.

The next milestone was the second arch, and I figured that once I got there the rest was all gravy—because you'd think going downhill is easier. Unfortunately, it's not. You actually have to exert more energy to keep your heart rate up, and your feet feel like they're going to fly out from under you; they're hitting the pavement a lot harder because of the momentum (it's also a good way to give yourself shin splints, which hurt like hell). "Keep going, you motherfucker," I yelled at myself. I wasn't far from the end. I focused on the trees at the end of the bridge, just five or so blocks away. "Just one more song and you'll be there, man. Don't fucking stop!"

In New York, the usual aromas are of garbage or various foods wafting up from nearby restaurants and hot dog vendors, but when I reached those trees, man, they smelled incredible. They reminded me of sitting beneath the walnut tree in my grandmother's backyard, eating watermelon as a kid. I discovered later that those trees only smell like that for about two weeks a year, when they're in bloom. On every other week, the only thing you can smell is the MSG coming from the dive spots in Chinatown. I'll never forget the way those trees smelled on that day; it's embedded in my memory, right next to Mom's homemade apple pie.

After kicking that bridge's ass, I threw my hands up in the air and looked to the sky. "Thank you! Thank you!" I called out. I'm not quite sure who I was thanking; I guess I was thanking myself.

In the months that followed, what I had thought was just going to be a one-time thing became a regular occurrence. I could feel my red Superman cape growing every time I ran my way from Brooklyn to Manhattan, or from Manhattan to Brooklyn.

CONQUERING THE BROOKLYN BRIDGE IN THE DEAD OF WINTER.

It was like I was running toward the person I wanted to be, and leaving all the things I didn't like about my life (and myself) behind me. With every footstep, I was shedding another insecurity, another distraction, and the effects of another three A.M. beer. With every footstep, I was closer to getting my life back, baby.

These days, if I somehow manage to go a whole week without running a bridge at least once, it's been a bad week. I've even had some of my most inspirational moments running high over the East River, soaking up the views of NYC. One summer afternoon, I was just entering the on-ramp when I noticed another runner out of the corner of my eye, and he was gaining on me. This guy looked like a pro; he had the body of a seasoned marathoner and some seriously expensive gear. I assumed he would blow right past me, and I picked up my pace a little just so I wouldn't be totally embarrassed and emasculated when he left me in the dust. But what happened next was fucking awesome.

He caught up to me and we ran together—side by side—for the entire length of the bridge. For those nine minutes, we were totally in sync. I listened to him breathe and clear his nose (when you're a runner, you know what it's like to get a lot of snot moving around in your sinuses), and I compared his breathing to my breathing. I glanced over a few times and watched the way he held his hands, checked to see if he was looking around, or looking at me. I listened to our feet rap against the pavement in time. It was almost like discovering that I had a long-lost twin brother! I had just never experienced anything like that before. When we got the end of the bridge, I went right, and he went left, and I waved, "Later, brother." I love knowing that there are millions of other runners out there, people who love to get out and kick ass just as much as I do.

I know that not everyone has the option to run over one of the most famous bridges in the world on their way to work (or wherever); I'm pretty lucky that I have such scenic and inspiring landmarks around to choose from. But even if you live in the middle of nowhere, you can find a milestone to shoot for—whether it's a park in the middle of town, or a walking path, or a lake. Find your own bridge. The more you run to it, the more you'll accomplish—and the more *new* goals you'll create.

TELL YOUR FRIENDS

When I first started running, my buddy Georgie (the same guy who could do sixty push-ups at a time) told me that he was running, too—about thirty minutes at a time, three times a week. I wasn't doing anywhere near that much running at the time. (I was probably putting in about fifteen minutes at a time, maybe two times a week.) In fact, I was totally jealous and annoyed when he told me how much work he was putting in. I hated him. I didn't think I'd ever get to that point. Now, I'm texting him about my regular seven- or eight-mile runs, or about the half-marathon I did the other day, and it pushes him to run even farther and faster. (Of course, Georgie also likes to smoke half a joint before he heads out for his thirty-minute jog. While I'm a huge advocate of "whatever works," I do not suggest smoking weed to get motivated for a run.)

In the beginning, all of my friends were party people; they didn't want to hear about anything that didn't have to do with a bottle of whiskey and three strippers. Besides Georgie, I didn't really have anyone in my life that gave a shit about working out. The only other person in my phone who was remotely interested in my quest to get sexy was my brother; he was a little overweight, too, and sick of it. And since all we ever talked about was baseball and how much I ran that week, he got more and more into working out. We challenged each other. No big brother wants their little brother to do anything better than they do, so we pushed each other to reach our goals.

I also started telling everyone around me—the girl behind the desk at the gym, the UPS guy, anyone that walked into my bar who was built but didn't look like a total meathead fuck—about my latest accomplishments in the gym and on the road. I was suddenly comparing workouts with those guys I used to hate because their arms were so shredded (but their arms didn't look as big as they used to, my arms were getting bigger). Since running and working out is basically all I talk about anymore, a lot of my buddies—even the party people—have become more interested in getting in shape, too. My point is, tell your friends about your workouts, and you'll motivate each other.

TURN UP THE VOLUME

I think I've made it pretty clear that I'm a rocker—always have been, always will be. Rock 'N' Roll makes me happy. And nine times out of ten, if I'm running with my headphones on, I'm listening to Iron Maiden. Their songs are long and energetic, and most of them are about huge feats of strength. They even have a song about running: "The Loneliness of the Long Distance Runner."

Rocky, if you haven't guessed, is another huge inspiration for me. I lose my shit every time I watch that movie. At the end, when his face is all beat to hell, and he's screaming for Adrian, and Paulie lifts up the rope to let her in the ring and she runs to him and they hold on to each other, I just cry my fucking eyes out every time. I even have a playlist that's just two songs: it's the "Theme from Rocky" and "Eye of the Tiger." Including both songs, it's about seven minutes long, so I often just set it to repeat and shoot for running one mile for every rotation. Of course, I can't always manage back-to-back seven-minute miles,

"EYE OF THE TIGER" WRITTEN ON MY HAND FOR INSPIRATION.

but I try. I also like to put on this playlist and do nonstop crunches until both songs are over.

Other bands I listen to quite often when working out are early Metallica, Slayer, Mötley Crüe, KISS, Zeppelin, and the Stones—you know, the usual shit. Anything fast-paced and heavy works for me, but I've noticed that my very best workouts usually happen when I've got something new to listen to on my iPod. Don't take your chances with whatever crap they're playing on the radio at the gym. Find music you really love, that really inspires you, and load up your MP3 player.

On the other hand, when you're out there running it can sometimes be just as inspiring to listen to your feet pound the pavement, especially if you concentrate on your breath pattern. When you're running, it's best to go with a 3:2 breath count ratio; inhale with the first three footsteps, exhale on the following two. (If you're running exceptionally fast, your body may instinctively switch to a 2:1 breathing pattern.) The first time I tried focusing on my breathing, I learned to really like running without music.

A good way to keep from getting bored is to periodically switch your breath foot; I like to do this every couple of miles. I just hold my inhale for one extra breath, switching the pattern to 4:3. If you're running with music, it can be very difficult to stick with this pattern. Instead, you can just breathe to the music, as long as you're listening to something fairly fast-paced. If you're into adult contemporary, however, I wouldn't suggest breathing along to Michael Bolton, because you'll pass out after a mile (although I would pass out after fifteen seconds, due to his shitty music).

Shit to Listen to When You're Running

Billy Joel: *The Stranger*
I listened to this record on repeat during a half-marathon along the West Side Highway in Manhattan. When I got home, I plugged it into the stereo and listened to it while I took a shower—I can't get enough.

Iron Maiden: *Powerslave*
The last two tracks, "Powerslave" and "Rime of the Ancient Mariner," are exactly what it takes to push you over the top.

"Rime of the Ancient Mariner," in particular, is long enough to crank out another mile and a half at the end of your run.

Also by Iron Maiden: *Somewhere in Time, Piece of Mind, The Number of the Beast, Fear of the Dark, Iron Maiden* . . . all of them are great to work out to.

Motörhead: *Ace of Spades*
This record will kick your ass from beginning to end—it never fails. Also by Motörhead: *Overkill.*

Mötley Crüe: *Too Fast for Love*
Packed full of big-hair sleaze to get you through even the worst hangover.

Airbourne: *Runnin' Wild*
These guys are just about the only new Rock 'N' Roll band you'll find me running to. Killer hooks and intelligent, greasy lyrics, plus a fast-paced tempo on every song.

AC/DC: *Highway to Hell*
This album is immaculate. If you've never heard it—from front to back—you should reevaluate your entire life.

Also by AC/DC: Everything they ever did kicks ass. Of course, their first singer, Bon Scott, died in 1980; later that same year they put out their biggest album, *Back in Black.* Any Bon Scott–era AC/DC song gives me chills.

Guns N' Roses: *Appetite for Destruction*
Don't make me kick your ass.

Queens of the Stone Age: *Songs for the Deaf*
This is their third album, which came out in 2002—a time when people had forgotten about Rock 'N' Roll, a time when rock music had given way to stupid hats and catchy pop songs with no bass players.

(continued)

The Rolling Stones: *Exile on Main Street*

This album came out at a time when the Stones were down on their luck—tax problems forced them out of their native England and they all moved to France. Because their management had sucked them dry (without their knowledge), they were practically broke. But how else could you write such an amazing album about hardship and self-pity when you're already the biggest band in the world? Put this record on and they'll be right there with you, as you force yourself to put one foot in front of the other.

Santana: *Santana*

Yes, he's been around since your parents were kids. But Santana didn't always feature a different pop singer on every song. In fact, he had a lot of songs with *no* singers. This album, from 1969, is a great way to switch things up if you get tired of metal. (If that's even possible.) I had an incredible time listening to this record in the dark, in a pair of sweatpants, very early on in my running career—it felt like a full marathon, but it was less than four miles.

The Sword: *Gods of the Earth*

This is the first album from one of the only decent modern metal bands, and it kills. From the first note to the last, this record will make you want to sweat your ass off, and throw a few punches along the way.

Metallica: *Kill 'Em All*

The first record from a huge force in metal, and in music. This record, with its well-crafted riffs, will melt your face off. I dare you not to play air guitar while you're listening to it. (It's not possible.)

Also by Metallica: Their first four records are impeccable. After that, press the "skip" button.

Slayer: *Reign in Blood*
It doesn't get any heavier than this. But if you listen to it carefully, you can hear that Dave Lombardo's drumming isn't much different from sped-up hip-hop, which makes this easy to stomp your feet to. If you feel like breaking shit—or getting rid of the fat around your waistline—put this in.

Also by Slayer: *Show No Mercy* and *South of Heaven*.

Steely Dan: *Can't Buy a Thrill*
This is great on a day when you don't need quite so much thrash and you just want a great song to hum along to. If you're taking a relaxed stroll in the park on a Sunday afternoon, this is the record.

Van Halen: *Van Halen II*
Why did I pick II? Because it's the first Van Halen album I ever heard and it's been my favorite ever since. I even did a cover of their cover of "You Really Got Me" in my junior high talent show. On top of all that, Diamond Dave loves to work out . . . and drink. My two favorite things.

ORGANIZED RUNNING

If you're at all interested in running (and in changing your life for the better), the best way to get started is to register yourself for a race. Don't be afraid of the word "race." It's not really a race unless you have 1 percent body fat and you're a freak of nature; it's just a group of people who would rather be out smelling the fresh air on a Sunday morning than eating doughnuts with their morning coffee. (Not to say that you can't have doughnuts after the run. On the contrary, you can totally have a doughnut and not feel guilty in the slightest.)

A 5K, for all you morons out there, is a five-kilometer run, which is just over three miles. You could probably go out and do one right now if you really wanted to. (You might find it somewhat miserable; you can even go on DRUNKDIET.com and send me hate mail if you like.) But if you sign up for one that's happening two months from now, you'll actually have a reason to get your ass out of the house and start training. All you have to do is get on the Internet, search for "running" in whatever town you live in, register, and then show up. Organized runs take place nearly every weekend in just about every town in the world. Trust me, it's an amazing experience, and it will completely change your life.

The first organized race I "competed" in was an 8K, which is just under five miles. Most people start out with a 5K, but with as much running as I'd been doing, I knew I was ready. Besides, this particular race fit perfectly within my insane schedule. Most runs happen on Saturday and Sunday mornings, which is just about the time I'm getting off work. The last thing I need to do is attempt five miles when I'm drunk, tired, and ready for bed. So, I kept checking the race schedules in my area, and I finally found one that wasn't on a weekend. It was Thursday morning, Thanksgiving, at nine A.M. in New Jersey.

The Sunday before the race, I mapped out a nice 8K run near my house. I'd actually run this exact route a few times before, I'd just never timed myself, and my goal was forty minutes—five eight-minute miles, though I was willing to settle for forty-five minutes, since it was only my first race. (And again, when I say "race," I don't mean that I was literally hoping to be the first to cross the finish line. I was going to be happy just to cross it at all.) It took fifty minutes to get through my practice run, but I knew the steep bridges and hills involved had probably slowed me down a bit. Since there weren't going to be any mile-and-a-half-long bridges in the actual race, I figured I'd come in pretty close to my goal.

This particular practice run also marked the first time that I had run that distance—actually, any distance—without stopping to walk. On every other run up to that point, I would bust my ass for a mile or so, then walk for the next thirty seconds to one minute to catch my breath. This time, however, I decided I wasn't going to stop, and I was willing to slow my pace to make that happen. I sure as hell didn't want to have to stop and walk like a pussy in front of all the other runners come Thursday morning. Registering for that first organized run, it turns out, was just the inspiration I needed to give up the walking; I wasn't about to look like an asshole in front of 1,000 strangers.

The very next morning, Monday, I ran to work. On Tuesday, I lifted weights as usual, and went back to the bar. On Wednesday morning, the day before the race, I dragged my ass out of my bed early, even though I'd only had about five hours of sleep. I knew it was going to be incredibly difficult to get up at 4:30 A.M. on the morning of the race if I didn't somehow get to bed early, so I ran some errands, grabbed lunch, and kept myself busy so I wouldn't end up taking a nap on the couch. Around six P.M. I went to the corner bar and drank tequila and beer for a few hours. Then I came home and made dinner, and watched *Rocky* for a while. I was asleep by ten P.M., which is absolutely unheard of for me. I woke up a few times during the night, but each time I'd push play on the DVD player, watch a few more minutes of *Rocky* for added inspiration, and fall back asleep.

When I arrived in New Jersey the next morning, I smoked a cigarette, ran around the block to warm up, stretched, and wondered how many of the 1,800 runners there had gotten drunk the night before like me. I took my place at the starting line, and it was amazing; there were people lining the sidewalks, cheering everyone on. I was so inspired to be among so many other runners. At the time, I only had two other friends who were into running; the rest of them stayed skinny by doing too many drugs and not eating enough, and it was refreshing to be surrounded by other people who had a passion for something just like I did. (Of course, I still wanted to kick all of their asses.) I finished the race in forty-one minutes, one minute over my goal. And when I crossed that finish line, I threw my hands in the air and smiled. There is just no greater feeling than finishing a run.

MY FIRST HALF-MARATHON IN MAY 2010.

What the fuck is a *Marathon*?
Marathon: A cross-country
footrace of 26.2 miles

So, the word "marathon" comes from an old Greek legend: In 490 B.C., after the Greek army defeated the Persians in the epic Battle of Marathon (which took place in—wait for it—Marathon, Greece), they had a soldier run all the way back to Athens to tell everybody about the victory. Apparently, this guy was so excited to break the news that as soon as he made it back to the city, he fell over and died . . . although there's some dispute about that. Either way, I find this story highly unlikely; I've gone running in Greece, and everyone looked at me like I was a crazy person who'd just robbed a bank.

The version of the race you're probably a bit more familiar with came about in 1896, when the marathon became an official event at the first modern Olympic Games. (No word on when the spandex panties became popular.) The women's marathon was added in 1984. And these days, there are hundreds of marathons happening every year, all across the world. Here's some other interesting shit to think about:

Full marathon = 26.2 miles
Half-marathon = 13.1 miles
Ironman Triathlon = 2.4-mile swim + 112-mile bike ride + 26.2-mile run

Sunday morning runs, by the way, are usually measured in kilometers.

10K = 6.2 miles
8K = 4.86 miles
5K = 3.1 miles

NEW GEAR

Back when I first started running, I'd only wear a Jack Daniels or an AC/DC T-shirt, and I quickly got to the point where I was running out of clothes. Plus, it's extremely uncomfortable to run around for forty-five minutes in a cotton shirt, dripping with so much sweat that it looks like someone just threw you in a lake. Running is not a fashion show—and the chances of running into anyone from your real life while you're out there are slim—so it's much better to be comfortable than it is to be fashionable.

Real running shirts, or "wicking" shirts, have a moisture-absorbing mesh that wicks away the sweat, which will keep you from feeling like a sweat-soaked mess midway through your run. For a man, jogging shorts are also a great investment. I have a pair with spandex boxer briefs built in that keep my junk from flopping around. (Sometimes it can get really annoying if you don't have something to hold the boys tight.) When it's not 1000+ degrees outside, I actually prefer to run in spandex pants; they're much more comfortable, and *way* more Rock 'N' Roll.

My dresser used to be filled with jeans and T-shirts, but I remember the day I decided to dedicate an entire drawer to running clothes. And these days, my apartment is so overrun with gear I don't know where to fucking begin. I own countless one-dollar *Rocky*-style stocking hats for winter running, but whenever I'm about to leave the house to do seven miles in 23 degrees, I can't seem to find any of them. I wind up running two miles to the guy that sells hats and gloves on the street and buying a new fucking hat. I also have twice as much laundry as before—so many piles of wet, smelly shirts and pants I can hardly keep track.

What the fuck is *Wicking*?
Wicking: To draw off
(liquid) by capillary action

If you go out running in a cotton shirt, all that sweat gets absorbed by the fabric but doesn't evaporate very quickly, leaving you wet, possibly cold (if there's a chill in the air), and probably smelly. A wicking shirt, however, pulls the moisture off your skin and helps it evaporate, so you feel dry and comfortable. In other words, a wicking shirt is a fancy name for a running shirt.

Workout gear is expensive, and each item you purchase should be considered a reward for something. Every so often I treat myself to some new gear, whether it's a running shirt, weight-lifting gloves, a different type of protein powder, or new shoes. Don't go out before your first run and spend $400 on gear. It's completely unnecessary to buy a wicking shirt if you're only putting in thirty minutes a week on the elliptical. Save the fancy stuff for later, when you actually need it (and you actually understand what the gear should be used for). Shoes, however, are a must-have. Go ahead and drop the $125 on some new running shoes.

The first time you go out to buy running shoes, you should find a local store that caters specifically to runners. Stay away from those sporting-goods chain stores that carry tennis rackets and kayaks. Chances are the guy working there has nothing on his mind other than clocking out at nine P.M. so he can go home and play computer games and jack off to You-Porn. You want advice from a real runner, working at a real running store, who runs more than five miles a year and can give you an accurate assessment of your running style and help decide what shoe is best for you. He'll put you on a treadmill with video cameras pointed at your feet, watch how you run, and play back the tape for you. Everyone runs different, and there's a different type of shoe for every type of runner. Trust your man at the running store, he knows what he's talking about.

Don't worry about going in with a specific brand or a specific color in mind. Most brands make different types of shoes for different types of running, and they make each of those types of shoes in lots of different colors. The guys who make real running shoes understand that we have to buy a new pair every three or four months, and they don't want us getting bored and switching brands because we're tired of wearing the same color year after year. Buy your shoes. Touch them. Smell them. Cherish them. Name them. Buy fancy running socks to put inside them. But remember, your new running shoes are only to be worn for running, not for trips to the grocery store.

You'll need to purchase new shoes every 300 to 400 miles. I know, I get anxious just thinking about *driving* 300 miles, the thought of running that far is unimaginable. But I did the math, and realized that I put in 300 miles in about four months. It's really important to toss them at that point, or save them for lifting weights; if you run in worn-out shoes you'll risk injury. Your knees and back will start to hurt, and you won't be able to figure out why. (If you start to notice this type of pain, check out your shoes.) So every four months, religiously, I buy a new pair of shoes. I stick with the same brand and style because I figure, if it ain't broke, don't fix it.

RUNNING INJURIES

Injuries are common when you're out there pounding the pavement—all that stress on your knees and hips eventually takes a toll. That's why you've got to give your body plenty of rest between runs; you've got to give your muscles, joints, and tendons time to rebuild and repair themselves. I did some research and found about 100 different experts who had about 100 different opinions about how much rest your body really needs—anything from "rest at least one day per month," to "wait at least forty-eight hours between runs." Which is why I say, fuck the experts. I don't listen to them, I listen to my body—I listen to my aches and pains.

According to *my* body, it's okay to go on back-to-back runs every once in a while, but for the most part, I like to rest a day between runs. Occasionally, I'll take a couple ibuprofens for knee and back pain. As much as I hate pills, an anti-inflammatory will speed up the repair process and get me back out there sooner. I also always keep a cold compress in the freezer (four of them, in fact), just in case any of my muscles or joints get a little strained. I also find myself visiting the foot care aisle at the drugstore pretty often. But sometimes, I just have to run through the pain. If I get a callus on my foot, for example, or if the pain in my right hip comes back, I push through it. My body will tell me when something isn't right. If I have to, I'll take a few days off.

None of this is relevant, by the way, unless you're really putting in the miles. If you're only doing five miles a week and you get a little ache in your knee, don't use that as an excuse to rest for five whole days, you pussy. Of course your knee hurts, you're actually using it for a change!

What the fuck is an *Ultramarathon*?
Ultramarathon: A cross-country footrace of any distance over the traditional marathon distance of 26.2 miles; typically ranging from 50K (31 miles) to 100 miles

Yes, you could actually run 100 miles, with other people, in an organized event. Ultramarathons often take place on a two- to ten-mile course, and participants run around it multiple times until reaching the target distance. There are also timed ultramarathons, where the clock is set to, say, twenty-four hours, and you just keeping running until time is up and you see how far you made it.

Twenty-four hours is an extremely decent time to complete a 100-mile run. Of course, there's a lot of stopping involved— to eat, piss, shit, and rest. These races are run at a considerably slower pace than a "regular" marathon—about half the pace of a half-marathon, actually. Also, they're (obviously) only for the clinically insane. Which is probably why I would love to do one someday.

TAKE THE RUN, NOT THE PILL

Every goddamn commercial that comes on while I'm trying to watch *The Price Is Right* is about some bullshit new drug for some bullshit new disease. Prescription drugs are a business, people. And business is fucking good. People watch these crappy TV shows, hear about some new "miracle" drug that will make you happy if you mix it with your antidepressant and your MAO inhibitor, and think they've found a cure for all their problems. It's the easy—but not the healthy— way out.

Anxiety attacks used to be a near daily part of my life. I'd be riding the subway, feeling like the train was about to crash, or like the walls were caving in on me, or I'd have it in my head that the guy sitting across from me had a gun and was about to unload on everyone in sight. Getting on an airplane was the most terrifying ordeal in the world. I would sit there in my tiny seat, my long legs rammed up against the seat in front of me, with one hand white-knuckled on the armrest and the other clutching the cigarettes in my pocket—if the plane was on its way down, I wanted to be able to light up one last time. Sometimes even riding in the back of a taxi would trigger an attack, too, and I'd be absolutely convinced that I was not going to make it home alive. (Although, in fairness, New York City cab drivers are out of their goddamned minds). I have not had one single panic attack, however, since I started running regularly. Running makes me happy.

On the other hand, one of my best friends in the world decided that was he depressed—and, to be honest, I really do think the guy was suffering—but he thought the answer was to get on all sorts of medications and start going to therapy. Within months, he was a completely different person—he would come to the bar and act like a total idiot. He'd have a few beers, even though he wasn't supposed to be drinking while taking his meds, and get completely out of line with the ladies, grabbing their asses, just being totally inappropriate. I had to throw him out on several different occasions for grabbing some random woman's tits. I'd try to have a conversation with him, and it was like he wasn't even there. He'd have this blank stare on his face, and he seemed just numb, like he didn't give a shit about anything. Before long, he lost his job—a really good gig that he'd had for ten years. And then he lost his woman. Now he just sits on his couch and drinks beer, and I never see him anymore. Sure, he thinks he's doing okay, he's all doped up on "happy pills." But I swear to God, you could call this guy up and tell him that his mother was abducted by the ghost of Hitler, and he wouldn't give a shit.

Now, of course, I understand that there are some people out there who have actual mental and emotional problems and in order for them to be normal and function in society they probably need a pill or two. (Whatever the fuck "normal" is.) I'm sure there's a guy out there, probably living a few doors down, who might end up chopping your head off while you're sleeping if he doesn't take his little blue pill every morning. This is a guy you want to make sure gets his prescription filled on time every month. But my point is, when the Mesopotamians invented the wheel in 3500 B.C., I'm pretty sure the first thing on their minds wasn't "Fuck, yeah. This will get us to the CVS faster so we don't have to walk fifteen miles to pick up our Klonopin!"

Some people choose to visit a doctor when things aren't going great and wind up taking antianxiety meds; they figure that pills must be the "cure" for their sorry lives just because a doctor prescribed them. Well, I'm not buying what they're selling. The government and the FDA are pushers, and the doctors are street-level dealers. I have some friends that are hooked on the prescription pain medication Oxycodone, which is just a genius fucking drug. Some big shots in suits got together and said, "We're losing billions on the streets to heroin. Let's figure out how to take out the impurities, jam it in a pill, and make it legal with a prescription." Same thing with the ADHD drug Adderall, which as far as I'm concerned is just a legal form of cocaine, and it's getting more and more popular every day. These drugs make the Man rich; meanwhile, old Average Joe feels pleased with himself for getting hooked on something that's been FDA-approved. For my money, I'd rather get the *il*-legal shit from the dealer posted up outside the corner drugstore. (Unless, of course, you have health insurance, then definitely stick with the legal shit. It's free, and you'll feel like you're on the Tea Cups at Disneyland.)

If you are depressed or have anxiety, first of all, stop feeling sorry for yourself, you fucking pussy. Everyone gets depressed. Second, get off your ass and fix your problems. You don't need a drug to release happy hormones—running does the exact same thing by releasing endorphins in your brain. In order words, running can make you high.

At some point, early on in my diet and exercise plan, I started thinking about all the things I didn't like about my life and made a list (being out of shape, of course, was the first thing on it). But the more I worked out, and the sexier I got, the more my problems just seemed to melt away. Whatever problems I might encounter throughout the day just don't seem like that big a deal after a run; I've already accomplished something so great and so badass that the small stuff doesn't much matter. The way I figure, if I can push myself for just thirty minutes, the entire rest of the day will be more rewarding and fulfilling than if I hadn't gotten my ass of the couch. It may be a hell of a lot easier to take a pill in the morning than it is to get out there and run three miles, but just like the song from *Rocky IV*, there's no easy way out. Take the run, skip the pill.

What the fuck are *Endorphins*?
Endorphins: Chemicals found in
the body that resemble opiates

Serious runners often describe feeling "high" after challenging themselves over the course of several miles, but for years doctors and other assholes weren't convinced that this feeling of accomplishment was actually based in science. More recent research suggests that a "runner's high," however, is an actual, medical phenomenon, and it's caused by a flood of endorphins released during bouts of strenuous exercise. Endorphins, which are chemicals that make you feel euphoric, happy, or coked out of your mind, are also released when you laugh, listen to good music, eat certain foods, and even when you have sex. You know what that means—going on a run feels (almost) as good as getting laid. Running will also make you look a hell of a lot better in bed. Trust me.

RUNNING IS LIKE AN UNNATTRACTIVE WOMAN

For a long time, I didn't know if it was okay to consider myself a "real" runner. Sometimes I even struggle with that now. Every time I read something about a really serious runner, I wind up feeling like such a novice that I'm not sure I'm worthy enough to call myself one. But listen to me right now: If you own a pair of running shoes and a "wicking" shirt, you're a fucking runner. It doesn't matter if you run five miles a week, or eighty-five miles a week, you're a fucking runner and don't let anyone tell you any different.

Who's to say what the right amount of running is per week? I say it's best not to worry about it—just put your fucking shoes on and go. Every day you're going to have a choice between your DVR and your Asics, but every time you unlock your front door after finishing a run, you'll know you made the right decision—and you'll feel like a badass.

Look, I know it's a lot easier said than done. If it was as easy as putting on your shoes, the streets would be packed with people jogging five miles a day, three days a week. Instead, the drugstores are packed. Running is hard. In fact, running is a lot like an unattractive woman—you really have to love her to keep her around. But over time, if you learn to love her, to cherish her, to realize her potential and discover how amazing she is deep down, you'll realize that she's a lot better for you than the supermodel.

Three years ago, I was chain-smoking cigarettes, piss-drunk, spending most of my free time in a La-Z-Boy watching reruns of *M*A*S*H*. I still get drunk and watch *M*A*S*H*, of course, that's my favorite show, but I simply could not imagine my life today without running. In fact, I thank the running gods every day for keeping me healthy enough to get out there.

I used to be satisfied with "just getting by." I worked hard at my job, but that was the end of it. I was content with coming home after a hard day's (or night's) work, and just drinking my ass off. If that's the way you live your life, that's okay; your boss will be satisfied with your performance until the day you retire. But running taught me that there's so much more out there. I was realizing that the more I ran, the less I wanted to get shitfaced and smoke cigarettes. The more I ran, the more my vices seemed to disappear.

Running is a lot like life, actually (prepare yourself for another stupid fucking analogy). You'll encounter steep hills and shitty sidewalks on your runs, just like you'll encounter obstacles throughout your life. The way I see it, you have three choices whenever you reach one:

A) Take a different route and avoid the hill
B) Give up and walk home
C) Kick that hill's ass, and prepare for the next one

Now, what's it going to be?

CHAPTER EIGHT

Practice Makes Perfect, Asshole

LÜC'S LAW: IF YOU'RE NOT SWEATING, IT DOESN'T COUNT.

Nowadays, even during really busy weeks at the bar, I work out at least five days a week. My current schedule begins on Monday—I run to work, which is about 3.4 miles. On Tuesday I hit the gym, and then alternate running and lifting every other day throughout the week. (If for some reason I have to skip a day, I get extremely cranky and irritable.) And on Sunday, I rest. With the amount of time I spend working out now, I *could* get a second job and buy a nicer apartment. I could rebuild the engine in my hot rod. I could go back to school. I could spend more time playing the drums. I could spend more time having sex. I could learn a second language. Or, I could sit around doing jack shit. Working out, however, is how I choose to spend my free time; it's good for me, and it makes me happy. If I'm not at the gym, I'm usually thinking about what I'm going to do the next time I'm at the gym. If I see someone running down the street on my way to work, I get jealous and wish it were me who was running.

How did I go from this lazy, drunk fuck who forced himself to run one pathetic mile a few times a week, to becoming the workout addict that I am to day? The only answer I have is that once I saw results—and started feeling good about how I looked for the first time in my life—I wanted more.

About halfway through my quest to become sexy, sometime in the summer of 2009, I decided to hang a calendar on my wall to keep track of my daily workouts; I'd jot down which group of muscles I had worked or how far I had run, as well as my speed and time. I also listed the amount of calories I had burned for the week, according to the numbers on my heart rate monitor.

At the end of the year—about five months after I started keeping track of my progress—I could see that I had *not* worked out for a total of forty-six days, which means I was averaging five workouts a week. I had burned well over 30,000 calories—just from running—and logged around 300 miles (about fifteen miles per week). In five months, I had also put on six pounds of pure muscle.

For the next three months, I hovered right around the same weight. However, my arms were much smaller than I wanted them to be, even though they were fairly toned and I could do a good amount of push-ups—I had gotten so hung-up on running and losing my gut that my interest in lifting weights had waned. I preferred to spend the time pounding the pavement and burning off as many calories as possible to get my body fat down. Even though doctors and other assholes say that the more muscle you have, the more calories you burn throughout the day, I didn't give a shit. The only thing I cared about was having a flat stomach. However, all that dieting and running suddenly wasn't working—I had reached another plateau. I knew that I needed to step it up at the gym and put on some muscle; I just didn't know *how* to do that. I needed a plan. I had taught myself how to lose forty pounds—I didn't think it should be that difficult to gain back ten of them.

A friend of mine told me that he could bench-press 180 pounds, eight times in a row. He's a real skinny fucker, and

I knew that he wasn't working out near as much as I was, but I hadn't bench-pressed anything in so long, I didn't know if that was a lot of weight or not. It turns out that it is. (For me, at least.) And whereas I had focused on lifting small weights and doing a lot of reps—not that that was a bad thing, it toned the shit out of almost every part of my body, except for the extremely annoying lower-stomach area—I hadn't even thought about putting up heavy weights.

I put in another call to my brother, Andy, and realized that heavy weights were definitely the way to go at this point (these days he works out with a bunch of meatheads and ex–football players who are only interested in getting as big as possible). So I decided to go with three or four sets of only eight reps—and that by the eighth rep of the fourth set, it should be damn near impossible to put the weight up. Maybe I wouldn't be able to make the eighth rep at all, maybe I could only put up six or seven.

I had also assumed that with all the running I was doing, I didn't need to work out my legs at the gym. I couldn't possibly have been more wrong about that. If you want to get in shape and burn calories all day long, you can't neglect your legs. Now I know that if your legs aren't ripped, the rest of your body won't be ripped either (not to mention the fact that the more toned your legs are, the farther you can run). Same goes for your back and chest. If you only work out your chest, it won't get any bigger—you have to work out your back, too, in order to support the chest muscles and keep the spine aligned. I had always avoided working out my back in the past; my back hurts enough as it is. Bartending is just really hard on your back, always having to haul heavy buckets of ice and standing around for long periods of time. I had always figured that if I added sore muscles to the mix, it would be a recipe for disaster. Newsflash, asshole: it makes more sense to work out those muscles at the gym so they can handle all the shit you put them through on a daily basis.

I kept pushing myself, day in and day out, and just two short weeks after switching to heavier weights, my friends started to notice: "Damn, bro, you're getting shredded," or "Wow, your arms are getting bigger. You look incredible." And, of course, all that effort is really worth it when I walk into a nightclub with the boys, find a table, sit down, take off my leather jacket, and watch all the girls in the room turn to me with a sparkle in their eyes.

PUSH IT TO THE LIMIT

Someone once told me that you're supposed to feel like you're going to throw up after every workout, and that sometimes—if you're really giving it your all—you *will* throw up. That's a little extreme—unless you're some kind of freak, or the Heavyweight Champion of the World—but it's something to keep in mind. There have been many times after a workout where I seriously felt like I was going to throw up for the next two hours, especially if I'd just pushed myself to the limit and run consecutive seven- or seven-and-a-half-minute miles. But it's true what they say: What doesn't kill you makes you stronger. I like to push myself to the point where I'm teetering on being taken out of the gym on a stretcher. I need to really feel the burn the next day. Don't fuck around when you're at the gym. Make it count, every single time you lift a stack of weights.

I know for a fact that when I'm working on a treadmill, in an environment with a controlled temperature, I'll start sweating shortly after the sixth minute of my run. (I figured that out way back when I was still running in shoes that were three years old.) If I don't start sweating until the ninth minute, I know I'm being a pussy and wasting my time. The same holds true when you're lifting weights. Those people who are glued to the TV at the gym really piss me off—I don't even think they realize that they're not pushing themselves. They'll hit the elliptical, break a sweat, and head out after twenty minutes, thinking they did their good deed for the week. They may even feel so good about themselves that they'll go home and eat half a gallon of ice cream. I know this because I used to be one of those people. I see them every time I'm at the gym.

If you really want to get in shape, my first suggestion is to get off the goddamn elliptical machine and get on the fucking treadmill. The elliptical is for people who want to make excuses, or people who have had an actual knee or hip replacement, or people who are over the age of sixty-five. If you don't have anything wrong with your knees and hips—and I mean something seriously, medically wrong, not just a few aches and pains here and there—there is no reason you should be on the elliptical. That machine is a cop-out. Get your fat, out-of-shape ass on the treadmill, burn some calories, and quit wasting time. Oh, and put down your fucking tabloid magazine while you're at it. You're at the gym, not sitting on your couch. Those people with the mega-ripped abs in that tabloid you're reading do not waste time on the fucking elliptical. They bust their ass on a treadmill, so that lazy people like you will spend money to see their sexy, no-talent ass on the big screen (while stuffing your face with buttered popcorn and gummy bears).

DON'T MAKE EXCUSES

There are a million excuses that will run through your head when it comes time to take a run or get in a workout:

- You're tired
- You're hungover

- You're hungry
- You didn't get enough sleep
- You don't have time
- You're waiting for your divorce to be finalized
- You're on your period
- You can't afford a gym membership
- You have to take a shit

These are all actual excuses that I've heard from actual ass-holes who have asked me for workout advice, by the way. Well, guess what? Working out is all mind over matter, and you have to overcome the excuses. For example, I make sure to take a piss right before I start working out so that the thought never even enters my mind—I don't want to have to interrupt my routine in any way for that one hour that I'm in the gym. There are twenty-three other hours of the day to take a piss, jerk off, eat cheeseburgers, or do whatever other stupid shit your brain comes up with. Remind yourself what your goals are: to get in shape, to look and feel amazing, to have more energy, to have a better sex life, to be the sexiest person you can be.

There are lots of things in life that you just don't have control over. Working out regularly, however, is something you can control. For example, maybe you're unhappy with your job and there's nothing you can do about it at the moment. You can, however, strap on your running shoes, go for a jog to clear your mind, and maybe even think of a way to change things for the better. Or, you could just sit on the couch eating junk food, growing more and more disinterested in your own life, and wake up tomorrow still not wanting to go to work. Your choice.

No matter how tired or hungover or pissed off I am, if it's

a day that I've scheduled to lift weights, I put on my goddamn sneakers and get my ass to the gym. Even if I screw around and don't break a sweat, at least I'm being consistent and staying in the habit of going. Of course, half-assing it in the gym will get you nowhere, and I am in no way condoning this behavior, but if it only happens once a month or so, don't beat yourself up about it. My point is, it's better to get your ass to the gym—even if you're dying of the worst Vegas hangover you've ever had—than it is to sit around on your fat ass watching TV. More often than not, I find that once I get to the gym, I'm inspired enough to get things done. And if not, I'll just do a light workout and be glad that I got anything done at all. I can't be fucking Superman *all* the time . . . just most of the time.

LEAVE YOUR PHONE IN YOUR LOCKER

One of the many things I've learned is that your mind has to be fully present when you're working out. Every rep, every set, every drop of sweat—you've got to be paying attention. You have to want to it, to need it. You've got to be hungry for it. Back when I was fat, however, I wanted to be anywhere but the gym. I'd bring my phone in there with me and find myself texting when I should've been moving into my third set. That's just completely counterproductive—resting any more than sixty seconds between sets isn't doing your muscles a bit of good. (Resting too long gives your muscles a chance to go back down to zero before pumping them up again. It's kind of like pumping the tires on your bike; if you pump once and then wait twenty seconds before pumping again, chances are you've lost more air than you've put in.) Sometimes I'd catch myself and think, *What the fuck are you doing? Does Kirk really need to know that you changed the oil in the hot rod today? Put the phone down, you bastard. Leave the video game in your locker!*

In case you were wondering, I often refer to my phone as a video game, because in an era when people have become more concerned with how many friends they have in their online community than with what's happening in the real world, texting has basically become a sort of reality video game. These days, lots of people seem to measure their self-worth by the amount of texts or tweets they receive; they will freak out if someone doesn't text or tweet them right back. It's like, if their inbox is empty for a whole five minutes they aren't pretty enough, or their father never loved them.

I'll admit it; I've had entire relationships with women via text. We'd joke, fight, fuck, and break up, all without having to actually see or touch each other. It's like having one of those handheld Nintendo devices, except the name of the game is "How much emotional damage can I cause this person without ever actually coming into physical contact with them?" My point is, there is absolutely no reason to have your phone beside you in the gym. The chicks can wait. While you're fucking around texting her, your heart rate is dropping and you're wasting time.

Sometimes on my walk over to the gym, my mind will drift from thinking about work, to girls, to doing the laundry, to paying the rent, to any one of the many stressful things that life throws at me on a daily basis. Then I catch myself and say, "Okay, fucker, for this one hour that you're at the gym, nothing else matters. Whatever happened at the bar last night, the fight I had with one of my friends, I can resolve that later. This one hour belongs to me and no one else."

FOCUS ON YOUR FORM

You know how every wall in the gym is covered in mirrors? They're not there for you to stare at how beautiful and ripped you are; they're there so you can monitor your form. I cannot stress proper form enough, by the way. It's much more important to do things correctly than to grab some heavy dumbbells and just go at it like a jackass. If you don't do the exercises properly, you're not doing yourself any good—you may even end up injuring yourself. It's actually better to use smaller weights, and to lift them slowly and correctly, than to grab the heaviest weight on the rack and kill yourself trying to lift it.

If you're trying a workout from a magazine or from something you found online, read the instructions thoroughly and consider the first time a practice session. If you decide to head to the gym and just wing it, don't be afraid to ask questions about how to properly perform a lift or an exercise. And by the way, if you're the type of guy who thinks women just want to get jackhammered as hard as possible when you take them to bed, before you roll over and go to sleep—you're exactly the kind of asshole I'm talking about. Otherwise, learn how to do things properly, and get the job done right.

BREATHE, DUMBASS

Sometimes when I'm doing an intense core workout, I forget to breathe correctly, or I'll forget to breathe at all. However, your muscles need oxygen to function properly. If you hold your breath while lifting a heavy weight, you're increasing your blood pressure—and if you're not careful you could wind up giving yourself a heart attack. So, inhale on the release, exhale on the lift. When you're doing a bench press, for example, inhale while you're bringing the bar down to your chest, and exhale as you push it back up. When you're doing crunches, exhale on the way up and inhale on the way down (when you pull yourself up, you'll need the extra room in your core). You have to breathe in and out with every repetition of every exercise to ensure that your muscles are getting enough oxygen to function. Trust me, I learned this shit the hard way. I used to do eight reps holding my breath, hoping to God my eyeballs wouldn't pop out of my head. Then one day I realized, Hey, dude, you can breathe while you're lifting. Genius!

What the fuck is a *Heart Rate Monitor*?
Heart rate monitor: A device that monitors your heart rate

Jesus, I didn't even have to Google the definition; this one's pretty self-explanatory. Just so we're clear, a heart rate monitor functions like a watch—you wear it around your wrist, and it has a strap that goes around your chest. That strap monitors your pulse, and sends the info to the watch so you can tell how fast it's beating. This comes in handy when you're running; if your heart is beating too fast, you'll burn out early. If it's not beating fast enough, you're not working hard. You can also get an expensive monitor with an embedded GPS—it'll tell you exactly how fast you're going, how many miles you've run, what time of day it is, which direction to head if you get lost. It'll even give you a blow job when you get home . . . Okay, so no blow job. But they do get pretty fancy.

THINK POSITIVE

A bit of advice: Think positively and positive things will happen to you. You know that friend of yours who is negative all the time? The guy who's always pissed off and thinks the world owes him something? Like a big pile of money should just magically appear in his apartment one day? Well, that guy's going to be broke and unhappy forever. Think about your other friend, the guy who is always happy, who has a good job, and a hot girlfriend or boyfriend, and a shitload of funny jokes to tell. If you don't have a friend like that, find one. And ditch the negative fucker, he's only going to bring you down.

CHAPTER NINE

Just Quit

LÜC'S LAW: STOP SAYING TOMORROW, OR NEXT WEEK,
OR WHEN I GET BACK FROM VACATION.
YOU'RE MAKING EXCUSES. DO IT NOW.

Back when I was a freshman in college, my buddy Ryan introduced me to a guitar player named Speers. Speers smoked cigarettes, and I thought this made him look cool as shit. So, in the back of his '92 Honda Civic, which we called the Blue Gill, I lit up for the very first time. The very next day, which just happened to be New Year's Eve, I went out and bought my first pack. I was now officially a smoker, and I loved every fucking minute of it. I smoked two packs a day for a little more than ten years.

When I first decided to get sexy, I figured there would be a day when I'd have to give up cigarettes for good. After all, you can't be shredded and still go out smoking and drinking every night (unless you're some kind of thoroughbred genetic freak). But I was dedicated; I was proud to be a smoker. Cigarettes made me feel like John fucking Wayne. I didn't care if they were fucking up my body. I was so tough, I didn't even care if I got cancer and died at fifty. But then my father managed to quit after smoking three packs a day for fifteen years, so that was a bit of an inspiration. (He didn't use the gum or the patch or anything, he just bummed smokes off his Army buddies for a few months—he's a Vietnam vet—until they got annoyed and stopped sharing.) And then I turned to Rocky.

I think I've made it clear that the *Rocky* movies are a huge inspiration to me. And way back at the beginning of the first *Rocky*, Stallone was a smoker and a drinker. But then Mickey told Rocky that he was going to have to quit that shit, and whatever Mickey says goes in my book.

Ultimately, I didn't quit because I was afraid of dying. I didn't quit because I wanted to save money (a pack of Camels is more than $12 in New York; if you do the math, I'm saving $700 a month). I quit because one day I was running over the Manhattan Bridge, and it hit me like a ton of bricks. I said to myself, "This is fucking ridiculous." I love running more than anything, and I knew that if I quit smoking those fucking things, I'd be able to run faster, harder, and longer.

I was a little over a year into my new running career, and up to that point I'd been smoking the whole time I'd been running. Not simultaneously, you asshole; I mean I would smoke a cigarette while I was lacing up my shoes and then run 3.4 miles to the bar, where I'd have a pack of cigarettes hidden in one of the cabinets, and light up again. (I had to hide them because everyone who works in a bar is a smoker; it's just part of the lifestyle. In fact, the best part of a shift is kicking everyone out at the end of the night and lighting up a cigarette and enjoying a shot and a beer, without having to serve any more drunk idiots.) I had gotten to the point, however, where I was realizing that it takes a lot more balls to, say, run a marathon than it does to light up a cigarette. Hell, I could smoke while watching *The Price Is Right*. I could smoke while taking a huge shit. Women can do it, teenagers can do it, and your mother can do it; what's so fucking tough about that? Smoking isn't tough. You know what's tough? Hill training. You know what's even tougher? Quitting. Quitting is tough. It is a hell of a lot harder to quit smoking than it is to keep lighting up every day until you eventually die a miserable, black-lunged, hairy-backed, greasy-faced, fried-banana-sandwich-eating, Elvis-on-the-shitter death.

Smoking is tough and sexy? Using that logic, you could argue that the local village idiot, the guy sitting at the end of the bar on a Tuesday afternoon with a cigarette hanging out of his mouth, is the toughest guy in the neighborhood. You know that guy—the one with his ass-crack hanging out, who hasn't shaved in six days, whose family won't talk to him, whose father disowned him when he was twenty-seven, who hasn't been laid in nine years, and whose only son won't claim him as a father. But by God he can drink more than you and he's proud of it! Doesn't look like much of a tough (or sexy) guy to me. In fact, one more beer and I could probably push him off the bar stool with my index finger. Look, it's more difficult to juggle tennis balls than it is to light up a cigarette, and I don't see too many jugglers getting laid on the boardwalk in Coney Island. My reasoning for continuing to smoke—that it made me seem tough and sexy—didn't make any fucking sense anymore, and it was time to do something about it.

So, my friend, that was it. I used the John Wayne method of quitting smoking. Of course, John Wayne didn't quit smoking—he died of a stroke—but I like to think that if he had, his approach would have been similar to mine. Which is to say I quit, cold turkey. I gave up a two-pack-a-day habit in March 2010, and I haven't had a cigarette since. I never had another drag, never bummed another smoke from a friend when I was shit-faced at four in the morning, never carried a lighter in my pocket, never smelled like stale cigarettes, never had smoker's breath, and never had another smoker's cough. . . . Okay, that last part's not true. When you quit smoking, your lungs are busy repairing themselves, so you hack up all kinds of huge chunks of nasty shit. It's enough to make you want to throw up. I would sit on the couch writing this very book with a fucking bucket next to me for all the chunks of shit I was coughing up. Painful, deep-down nasty coughs that were enough to make the neighborhoods wonder if I was dying of emphysema. That, combined with severe crankiness and food cravings that made me want to kill everyone around me and break everything in my apartment. In fact, it's enough to make you want to light up another cigarette. But that's not how I do things.

I realize there are lots of people out there who are struggling to quit. And I don't mean to make it sound easy; it was fucking hard as hell. Most of the shitty stop-smoking Web sites said that the first three days were going to be the hardest. So I made those three days the focus of my entire life. I didn't care about next week or next month, all I cared about was the next hour. I counted down every single hour of those next three days one by one. When it comes to difficult things, thinking about the big picture actually makes them more difficult. For example, when you're running a marathon, you can't think about the whole twenty-six miles or you'll drive yourself insane and give up. You think about mile three; you focus on that mile and the accomplishments you made within that mile only. Then it's on to mile number four, and number five, and so on. So when I quit smoking, I didn't focus on the whole three days, or the whole seventy-two hours. I focused on one hour at a time, the hour I was living at that very moment. Every hour was like its own adventure; you have to enjoy (or endure) the adventure you're on right now.

I quit on a Monday. On my way to work, I stopped at the

drug store and blew $60 on nicotine gum. I chewed a piece and went about my day, trying not to think about smoking—I ordered food, I ate some peanuts, and I counted a lot of other people's money at the bar (that helped). Anything I could do to keep my mind, my hands, and my mouth busy, I was doing it. When I got home, I chewed another piece of gum and then I thought to myself, *Hey, you pussy. If you're going to chew this fucking gum, you might as well light up another cigarette. Either you're fucking in or you're fucking out—which is it?* It was eight P.M., so I decided to do something that was going to either make me or break me—I went to my corner bar.

You hear all these people say things like, "I only smoke when I'm drinking," or "I used to smoke a lot, but now I only smoke when I drink." So I drank as much as I normally did and I'd go outside with everyone else when they went for a smoke break—I just didn't smoke. I toughed it out, chewing bar straws the whole time, telling myself that it would get easier. I did that until about two A.M., until I was drunk enough to pass out without thinking about smoking while rolling around in bed. Probably not the healthiest way to handle the situation but fuck you, it worked.

The next day I woke up, ate breakfast, and went straight to the gym for a good two hours. Then I came home, got ready for work, and went to serve assholes cheap beer for nine hours. I talked to everyone at the bar about the fact that I was quitting smoking. I called everyone I knew and offered them free beer to come hang out and talk to me. I walked outside every hour and breathed in the fresh air as deep as I possibly could, and kept telling myself that the clean air was much better for me than the smoke-filled air I'd been breathing for ten years. Clean air is a gift from God—and trees—and I was ready to stop taking it for granted. I did some more shots and chewed through about 400 bar straws and went home piss-drunk, again. Two days down, one to go.

By day three, as much as I wanted to kill myself, I did not want to smoke. I found some comfort in the fact that by tomorrow, the cravings weren't going to be as bad. Maybe that's because I had set my mind on the fact that on day four, everything was going to be easier, but the mind is a very powerful thing. Also, who gives a fuck? It worked. I slept in late, woke up, and went for a run. After all, that was the main reason I was quitting—to run longer, faster, and harder. To be a better man today than I was yesterday.

Those three days might have been the hardest three days of my entire life. And on my deathbed, when I think back about all my accomplishments, all the marathons I will have run, all the books I will have written, all the jokes I will have told, I'm pretty sure that those three days will remain at the top of the list of difficult shit I did. I learned a lot about myself during those three days. For one thing, I'm a lot tougher than I gave myself credit for. At the same time, only a complete idiot would have put himself in that position to begin with.

No matter how you decide to do it, quitting is going to be fucking hard as hell. I had been a little nervous about those rumors that quitting makes you gain weight; the last thing I needed was to gain back all the weight I'd lost. So I ate baby carrots by the handful because they were somewhat shaped like cigarettes and wouldn't make me blow up like a fat balloon. (Though it did occur to me that cigarettes—and baby carrots—are rather phallic. Why would I want all these things shaped like small cocks so close to my mouth?) I also gave up chewing gum, which is perhaps counterintuitive. (Lots of people turn to gum to quit smoking.) In the past, I wouldn't leave the house without a pack of Camel Lights and a pack of Dentyne Fire; if I wasn't smoking, I was chewing gum. But I gave it up for two reasons: (1) I equated gum chewing with smoking, and (2) I decided that gum manufacturers just cannot be trusted; all those artificial ingredients and crap you can't pronounce—it's a turnoff. Now, I've replaced the gum and my little white cancerous friends with toothpicks; cinnamon-flavored toothpicks, actually. (I still wanted something to put in my mouth, and I needed something to keep my breath fresh.) You can't be shredded if you're out drinking and smoking every night, which is why toothpicks are the new cigarettes (and they still make me look pretty tough). Come on! Nicky Santoro looked pretty badass in *Casino*, didn't he?

After about three days of pure hell, all those feelings of anger and frustration started to turn into thoughts of pride and accomplishment. Quitting was easily the best decision I ever made in my life. I have decided, however, that it's okay for me to smoke the occasional cigar when I'm raising hell in Vegas. Surprisingly I can smoke a cigar every now and then, and still have absolutely no interest in cigarettes. I do, however, have this recurring dream that I smoked a cigarette at a party, and then I wake up pissed off and disappointed in myself. Luckily, that's just a dream and it didn't happen. And it didn't happen because I'm a fucking champion—and champions don't smoke cigarettes.

CHAPTER TEN

What I've Learned

LÜC'S LAW: YOUR BODY IS A FULL-TIME JOB.

O ne night I was sitting in my bar, wondering why I couldn't just get drunk all day, eat like shit, get wasted, and repeat. Why wasn't the human body designed to have fun *all the time*? Why must we contend with hangovers and boredom? And then, after careful consideration, I figured the answer to that is actually pretty simple: If we partied every day, all day, partying just wouldn't be that fun anymore. Once I got my shit together, I also realized that partying—if that's all you ever do—is an empty, meaningless way to live. Sure, if I kept getting shit-wasted every night, I'd have some great stories to tell by the time I turned fifty, but I'd also be that creepy old dude in the local corner bar, the crusty guy drinking whiskey at four P.M. on a Tuesday, telling those same fucked-up stories to people who've already heard them three times before. It's all fun and games when you're twenty-five, but no one wants to watch an old, fat, drunk guy with BBQ stains on his T-shirt try to chase tail. Even Fonzie got old (and these days he's really just a nerd with a big nose and gray hair).

When I think back to those nights when I would go out and get completely shit-faced, it just seems so pathetic. I'd get so upset if I couldn't find a girl to come home with me that

I'd wind up taking home a Borracho instead. (Even though the truth is, I could have gone home with a different girl every night. But that's just not my style. I wanted *my* girl, not some coked up dump truck.*) I'd go home every night alone and miserable, and no one wants to be around someone who's pissed off and grumpy all the time.

The only thing worse than the nights I took home a Borracho were the nights I really let myself run wild, the nights that a few extra drinks after work turned into an honest to God bender. And before I got my life together, there were a lot of those nights—more than I care to admit. Whenever I felt like maybe I wasn't getting enough attention, or maybe something in my life wasn't working out the way I wanted, I'd get shit-wasted and piss away money on booze and blame it on everyone else but myself. Instead of turning to my friends for help, I'd lash out at anyone who got in my way. I mean, it couldn't possibly be *my* fault that I was drunk and broke . . . even though I had been the one ordering double-shots of Jameson for twelve hours straight. It had to be my girlfriend's fault, for not spending enough time with me. Or my friend's fault, for giving me the password to the hotel room safe (and access to the last bit of cash I'd locked away). I suppose this was my fucked up way of getting the people in my life to show me that they actually cared. I'd push them all farther and farther away, just to see who was left standing. If I hadn't been drunk and miserable all the time, I wouldn't have needed that kind of validation. But since I was drunk all the time, I'd throw tantrums when I didn't get my way, like a nine-year-old boy at

---

*Dump Truck (dump trək) N. Female.

  1. A total slut with no class.

  2. A truck with a bed that may be tilted to discharge its contents through an open tailgate.

"I can't believe you took home that dump truck last night. You better change your sheets."

his older brother's birthday party. I'd dodge calls from my family, and act like an asshole to my friends. *If no one wants to give me any presents*, I thought, *then I'll make them sorry.* But it was always me who'd end up feeling sorry . . . especially on those days that I'd wake up alone, faced with a staggering hangover, an empty wallet, and zero messages on my phone. I didn't want to keep hurting the people I loved most. I didn't want to live like that anymore. I didn't want to be a drunk asshole.

I'm not real big on psychology or thinking about feelings and all that bullshit, but I did decide to take a serious look at my life. Why was I raising so much hell? Well, because it's fun as hell, that's why. But I also think it's because I was unhappy. I was unhappy because I was overweight. And the "medicine" I was using to alleviate this unhappiness was only making me fatter and more depressed. And then all of those feelings that I had buried inside finally came out, *with a vengeance*—I started using those feelings and those insecurities to push myself to become what I had always wanted to be: the sexiest man on the planet.

There's a reason that so many people in this country are overweight and just can't seem to drop the pounds: because it's fucking hard. Losing weight and getting in shape takes a lot of time and a serious amount of discipline, willpower, and self-control. And let's face it, if we all had a lot of willpower and self-control, we wouldn't have gotten fat in the first place.

I spent ten years of my life wishing—wishing that I was skinny, wishing that someday I wouldn't be embarrassed to take my shirt off in front of a girl, wishing that someday I'd be able to have sex with my shirt off, wishing that someday I would like what I saw when I looked in the mirror. I was 200 pounds, and I spent most days sitting around on my fat ass with no purpose, killing the hours (and stuffing my face) until it was time to go back to work. Every winter I would say, "This is the year. When summer rolls around, I'm going to be sexy. I'll be able to go to the beach and feel good about how I look." But for ten years, that didn't happen.

Lots of us do this—sit around wishing and waiting for some kind of miracle to happen. For me, it was almost as though wishing and waiting were just part of life, that *doing* something wasn't really an option. It took digging down deep inside of myself and scooping out whatever inspiration I could find to make the changes that ultimately got me where I am today. But change doesn't happen easily, and if you start to think about tomorrow, rather than today, you're setting yourself up to fail. Think about right *now*. Think about this day, this hour, this minute. When I quit smoking, for example, I didn't think about tomorrow. I thought about how miserable I was and how much phlegm I was coughing up out of my damaged lungs. I looked at the clock and patted myself on the back every time the minute hand reached 12. When I'm on a six-mile run, I don't think about the sixth mile. I think about the mile I'm on right now, about putting one foot in front of the other. If you're thinking about the finish line, or about how good it would feel to stop, about catching your breath, or Chinese food, or taking a piss, you'll never make it past the first mile. Think about how far you've already come, not how far you have to go. Put a towel over the computer screen on the treadmill. Put a piece of tape over the total distance on your Garmin. Learn to love vegetables because they make your body feel better, your clothes look better, and the mirror friendlier. Tell yourself that every piece of bread you turn down puts you one step closer to your goals. No one else is going to give a shit, by the way, if you eat a piece of bread or not. No one is going to pop out of the bathroom at the restaurant to pin a medal on your chest because you told the waitress to hold the fries. You have to do it for yourself. You have to be your own inspiration. It *is* possible to eat a cheeseburger without French fries. It *is* possible to eat a burger without cheese. Your testicles will not be removed if you order broccoli instead of potato salad. On the contrary, your sack will actually feel better when you can fit in those jeans that have been hiding in your closet since college. Take life one meal, one hour, one mile, one job-well-done at a time.

My priorities have changed completely since I found this new love for taking care of my body. I actually have things to look forward to, like the 300-mile charity bike ride from Boston to New York that I rode in September 2010, and the marathons and half-marathons and 5Ks and 10Ks and every other run I do day in and day out. Now that I've lost forty pounds (and gained back fifteen in muscle), I'm excited to get up and take on the day. In fact, I'm usually so eager to hit the gym or go for a run that I pop right out of bed, put my shoes on and go. Every morning, I'm so fucking proud of myself and so happy, I feel like I can accomplish anything.

You know what else I've discovered? When you're sexy and confident—and you feel good about yourself—people take you more seriously. You become the guy everyone wants to hang out with. These days, my bar gets so packed on nights that I'm working, we have to stop letting people in at a certain point. I'm not saying that's just because I look amazing. It's mostly because I'm in a much better mood—I really want to be there, and I really want everyone to have a good time. As a result, other people really want to be there and really want to have a good time, too. That vibe comes through as soon as you walk in the door. It's a fun and joyful place (and not just because of the booze).

Even my friends have changed a lot over the last year or so. I used to be friends with dudes who rarely went to work, could barely make the rent, and just had an overall negative outlook on life. Most of them wound up in rehab (which worked for some and not for others). In fact, I'm the only one who has managed to control my alcohol consumption. The rest of them slowly started disappearing into Sober Land, or spiraling deeper into addiction.

I still love those guys, of course, I'm just much more interested in hanging out with people who have good things to say and exciting stories to tell. Think about it: Do you want to call your friend and listen to him bitch about how he hasn't gotten laid in three months, or how he smoked weed and played online poker all day? Or would you rather listen to a buddy tell you about the date he had with a smoking hot chick, or how much he loves his job, or that he's about to go for a four-mile run?

None of this means that staying in shape or eating healthy foods is easy, by the way. Partying, for me, is still an addiction. I'm not an alcoholic—I'm a partyholic. I love putting on a KISS record, drinking an entire bottle of wine, and spending an hour doing my hair before going out on the town. And even though I always end up wearing the same T-shirt and jeans, I'll try on four different shirts first, since I want to look my best. Back when I was fat, I really only had one shirt that didn't make me look (and feel) like a bloated bastard. Every overweight person understands this; you have one or two outfits that you feel comfortable in, that make you look a little bit more like the person you *wish* you were. Of course, now that I've gotten sexy, it's a lot more fun to try on clothes—I can basically wear anything I want!

As I was saying, partying for me is an addiction, and sometimes it gets the best of me. It's a constant battle to stay in with a book or my remote control on any given night, especially now that I have a shredded body to show off. But I keep reminding myself that the more often I stay in, wake up rested, and work out hard, the more fun I'll have the next time I go out. And, actually, it's much more fun to go out once a week—or even once every other week—than it is to go out every single night. If I go out drinking two nights a week, on top of the three nights I'm drinking at work, I just get run down. I can't work out as hard at the gym, I wind up feeling bloated and cranky, and I spend way too much money on the booze. Nowadays, partying has become more of a once-in-a-while thing than an every-night thing. And I know that the reason I'm in such good shape is because I've slowed down. You realize that as you get older, your body changes; it can't keep up like it used to, so your priorities have to change, too.

My mantra in life has always been: I want more, and I want it right now. More booze, more sex, more money, more food, you name it. Whatever I have in front of me usually isn't enough. Even now, I have to make a conscious effort not to overeat; sometimes that doesn't work out. I fucking love to eat. A friend of mine once told me that she'd never seen anyone consume as much food as I can. And it's true, no matter what or how much food you put in front of me, I won't stop until it's gone. If I was at a BBQ or—God help me—an all-you-can-eat buffet, I'd just keep eating and eating as if it was my last meal. I still struggle with this. I have to remind myself, "Hey, man, there will be many more meals after this. There's no reason to stuff your face until you have to unbutton your pants and take a nap."

I'm sure a doctor would tell me I have some form of OCD or some other bullshit; then he'd probably hand me some pill to "cure" me of my disorder. I say, fuck that crap. Maybe I just want more of everything, maybe that's just how I am. What's so wrong with that? True, it took me thirty years to understand this addiction, or affliction, or whatever you want to call it, but these days I use it to my advantage. I focus all that energy on positive things, rather than getting wasted. Instead of being addicted to booze and food, I'm addicted to working out and being healthy.

As soon as I got addicted to running, in fact, I didn't want to stop. I wanted to go farther and faster than I did the last time I was out there. I wanted to lift more weights and do more reps than I did the last time I was at the gym. Before long, it started to feel like I was scheduling work around working out, instead of the other way around. The drawers in my dresser were slowly being taken over by running shirts and compression pants. I actually learned to enjoy telling myself "no." And I accomplished what I set out to do: Despite what the books, experts, and other assholes say, I lost forty pounds while drinking whatever the fuck I wanted—it just turns out that I don't want to drink quite as much as I used to.

Sometimes I still find it hard to believe how much I've fallen in love with working out—though I don't consider myself to be a workout freak, like most of those assholes that you see in magazines with the six-pack abs and the shaved chests. By the way, when did shaving your chest become the "in" thing to do? Why would you spend so much time pumping up your muscles to look like some big tough guy, and then go and shave your chest and wax your armpits? Why not just chop your balls off while you're at it? I don't want to look like a twelve-year-old girl; that's disgusting. I'm proud of my chest hair, and I will never shave it off.

Anyway, I work out five to six days a week. When I'm seventy-five years old I hope I'm still lacing up my running shoes and cranking out a few miles. The hard part, of course, is getting to that point. You just have to stick with it. Find your own inner Rocky, your own Iron Maiden. Find inspiration wherever you can, and keep putting on your goddamn running shoes and hitting the pavement.

I used to think that Rock 'N' Roll was about getting fucked up every night and throwing televisions out of windows. Now I know that there's nothing more Rock 'N' Roll than partying all night (without getting completely out of control), making out on the dance floor, and then waking up and putting on your running shoes to go suck in all that fresh morning air. In fact, some of my biggest Rock 'N' Roll heroes are huge workout freaks. Take David Lee Roth, for instance. He started doing kung fu when he was twelve, and he's pretty handy with a sword. He's also an avid runner, and yet he still drinks like a fish. I even got him drunk back when I worked at the taco shop; he liked to come in and eat a few cheap tacos and drink Bud Lights. (He had moved to New York to become an EMT. That's right, there was a time when, if you passed out drunk on the street, Diamond Dave might have shown up to give you CPR. Sign me up for that!)

I realize now that there is no future in being drunk. Not that I'll ever *stop* drinking, of course, I'll never become one of those assholes who doesn't drink because he's too worried about his figure. (Frankly, I don't trust people who don't drink. There is just something not quite right about a guy who can't relax and have a beer; I wouldn't leave a guy like that alone in my apartment for two minutes.) But there comes a point in your life where you have to grow up.

These days, I know that all of my hard work in the gym and

on the road is going to waste with every drink that I order, and every once in a while I start feeling guilty for drinking, for consuming empty calories that my body doesn't need. Whenever I start feeling like that, I take a few days off from the booze.

I ran my first full marathon in Las Vegas on the morning of my thirtieth birthday. I held a pretty steady pace, running an average of nine-minute miles. Somewhere around the 25K mark, a whole bunch of cheerleaders were lining the route, dressed up as Gene Simmons and Paul Stanley and dancing around to KISS songs. (That was my fastest mile of the race: 8:32, and I gave every single one of those KISS girls a high-five.) Mile 24, on the other hand, was the hardest. My body was depleted of every form of fuel, there was no one around to cheer me on, and everyone around me was stopping to walk; though I suppose that means I paced myself a bit better than most of the remaining runners, which is pretty fucking cool.

FINISHING MY FIRST MARATHON ON MY THIRTIETH BIRTHDAY IN LAS VEGAS, DECEMBER 2010.

I've never been the type of person that wants things to be handed to me. In fact, I've been known to turn down opportunities that other people would kill for. That's because I need to feel like I've earned everything that I have, not like I just got lucky. And I think that's why I love running so much—it never gets easy. Every day is a fucking struggle, a bitch of an uphill battle. But that's the thing about the greatest things in life—you have to work for them. The greatest things in life are victories.

When I finally crossed the finish line—3 hours and 54 minutes later—my entire family was there waiting for me, and everyone was wearing a Lüc wig. I hugged my mother, shook my father's hand, and the whole crew headed off to find me a bathroom and a bar. It was actually the greatest birthday of my life, and I know they're only going to get better from here. Working out, running, and learning to eat right helped me get my body—and my life—back.

Lüc's Recipes

Here are just a few easy-to-make meals that I have managed to perfect on my quest to get sexy. Put these recipes in your regular rotation, and you'll get sexy, too. Rather than include actual nutritional information, I've rated these recipes on my patented Bullshit Meter—a "1" is superhealthy and supereasy to prepare, a "10" would be something that's not that healthy and a big pain in the ass to make (which is why none of these recipes actually rate a "10.")

BREAKFAST & LUNCH

LÜC FOO-YOUNG
SERVES: *2 people*

Ingredients:
  5 egg whites
  ½ bag frozen stir-fry vegetables (Make sure you buy the kind without any additives. The package should say "Ingredients: Vegetables.")

Separate five eggs (turn to page 88 if you can't remember how). Then, spray an omelet pan with a little organic olive oil—you'll use less oil with a spray can than if you pour it out of a regular

(continued)

bottle—and add the egg whites and the frozen vegetables. Cook on medium heat for about 8 minutes, or until the egg whites stiffen.

BULLSHIT METER: 1. Zero fat, hardly any carbs. Breakfast of champions.

HARDBOILED WHITES
SERVES: *You, for several days*

Ingredients:
Eggs

Grab a pot, and fill it with water. Put 6 to 12 eggs in there (depending on how big your pot is). Put the pot on the stove on high heat and bring the water to a boil. When it really starts boiling, move the pot off the heat and put a lid on it. Wait 12 minutes and you're done—breakfast for days. Just don't eat the yolk; it's nothing but fat and cholesterol.

BULLSHIT METER: 1

LÜC'S TUNA SALAD
SERVES: *2 people* (two wraps or two sandwiches)

Ingredients:
2 cans tuna packed in water ("Ingredients: Tuna, water"; no salt, no oil, no additives)
1 very ripe avocado

(continued)

¾ tablespoon Omega-3 oil (available in the refrigerated
   section of your local health food store)
Fresh cracked black pepper
Optional: Ezekiel 4:9 live-grain bread or tortilla

Empty the two cans of tuna into a bowl. Then, slice the avocado
in half, get rid of the pit, and scoop out the meat with a spoon;
add to tuna. Squirt in a little Omega-3 oil (you could also use a
little olive oil), grind some pepper on it, and mix that shit up.

If you'd prefer to eat your tuna salad in a wrap or as a sandwich, then use the live-grain bread. Throw the bread in a
toaster first and you'll feel like a fucking gourmet chef.

BULLSHIT METER: 2; 3 with the bread

LÜC'S GREEN SALAD
SERVES: *1*

Ingredients:
   Romaine lettuce (buy the prewashed kind in a bag;
      much easier)
   1 cucumber, sliced
   1 tomato, sliced
   Black or green olives
   2 hardboiled egg whites
   Olive oil
   Balsamic vinegar

Get a decent-sized bowl and throw all this shit in there. The key
to this "salad"—if you're a guy like me, anyway—is to throw as

(continued)

much healthy shit in there as you can to avoid the fact that you're actually eating lettuce. Cucumbers and tomatoes cost next to nothing, and you can find fresh olives in almost any grocery store. Just stay away from the canned shit (too much salt). Top this off with a little bit of olive oil and some balsamic vinegar, and you're one step closer to sexy. Eat one of these per day for a week, and I guarantee you'll notice a difference in your waistline.

BULLSHIT METER: 1

DINNER

LÜC'S SURPRISE

SERVES: *It's enough food for a week*

Ingredients:

- 1 green pepper, chopped
- 1 yellow pepper, chopped
- 1 red pepper, chopped
- 1 sweet onion, chopped
- 1 tablespoon organic olive oil
- 1 pound ground turkey
- 2 cloves garlic, minced (or cut up really small)
- 1 package sliced mushrooms
- 1 jar no-sodium marinara sauce
- Fresh cracked black pepper
- *Optional:* any dry spices you want, like cumin, Italian seasoning, cayenne pepper, or red pepper flakes
- *Optional:* two cups whole-wheat penne or macaroni

Throw the peppers and onions in a big pot with a little bit of olive oil and let them sit there over medium heat. In a separate pan over

(continued)

medium heat, brown the turkey (which literally means just let it turn brown. Stir it around a little bit and, when there's no pink left, it's done). Add the garlic to the pan with the peppers and onions and continue cooking for one minute. Then, add in the turkey, the sliced mushrooms, the jar of marinara sauce, and fresh cracked black pepper to taste. (At this point, you can also add any dry spices you want.) Cook until the peppers are done to your liking.

If I'm going through all this trouble to make food, it damn well better last me a week. So I put one serving on a plate for dinner, and the rest gets divided into four sandwich bags or plastic containers. Sometimes I'll boil a couple cups of whole-wheat penne or macaroni and throw that in there, too. It reminds me of Mom's goulash, without all the fat ass.

BULLSHIT METER: 4; 5 with pasta (This recipe rates a "4" because there are dishes to clean; the carbs in the pasta push that to a "5.")

FAKE SPAGHETTI
SERVES: *1*

Ingredients:
- 1 package tofu shirataki
- 1 cup no-sodium marinara sauce

Open the package of tofu shirataki and plug your nose—this stuff smells terrible. It's also like eating air; it has no calories, no fat, no nothing. It will fill you up, but it has no nutritional value. In fact, a runner died during a marathon because all she ate was shirataki. I'm not advocating you eat it all the time, but it comes in handy when you feel hungry but you've already eaten enough for the day.

(continued)

Wash off the shirataki, put it on a plate, cover it with the sauce, and throw that shit in the micro for 2 minutes.

BULLSHIT METER: 0

MOM'S SLOW-COOKER DRUNK DIET STEW

SERVES: *Enough to feed an army*

Ingredients:

2 pounds bison meat (or, if you're a pussy, you can sub in regular beef)

5 carrots, peeled, chopped

1 sweet onion, chopped

3 stalks celery, chopped

4 whole tomatoes, chopped

¾ cup water

½ cup quick-cook tapioca

1 whole clove

2 bay leaves

7 whole baby new potatoes, quartered

fresh cracked black pepper

Throw all this shit in a slow cooker on low for 10 hours. Your house will smell amazing for two days. Remove the bay leaf before serving.

BULLSHIT METER: 4 (there's chopping involved)

MOM'S PORK CHOPS WITH ORANGE BROWN RICE

SERVES: *Four people, or one person for four days*

Ingredients:

- 1 cup uncooked brown rice
- 1 cup sliced mushrooms
- 2 cups orange juice
- ¼ onion, diced
- 4 boneless pork chops (or, if you'd prefer, boneless, skinless chicken breasts)

Preheat oven to 325 degrees. Combine the rice, mushrooms, orange juice, and onions in an oven-safe casserole dish (the kind with a lid). Place the pork chops down in the rice. Put the lid on, and put it in the oven. After 30 minutes, remove the lid (to crisp the rice), and put the dish back in the oven. Cook for another 50 minutes.

*If you're substituting chicken for pork chops, the meal will cook for 1 hour total.

BULLSHIT METER: 6

CHICKEN AND VEGETABLES IN THE STEAMER

SERVES: *It really depends how much you put in the fucking steamer, doesn't it?*

Ingredients:

- 2 boneless, skinless chicken breasts
- Any vegetables of your choice
- 1 cup baby belle mushrooms

(continued)

Put the chicken breasts in the steamer and set the timer for 35 minutes. Add the vegetables when appropriate. (Broccoli cooks for 12 minutes, asparagus for 10, cauliflower for 12; the steamer comes with a chart on how long to steam different foods.) There's nothing to this. Turn it on and throw shit in there.

   I will admit that this does not have a ton of flavor, but it's healthy as all hell. I lived on this meal for like six months straight.

BULLSHIT METER: 1 or 2 (sometimes the steamer can be a little tricky to clean)

ROCKET FUEL

ROCKET FUEL
SERVES: *1*

Ingredients:
   1 scoop chocolate-flavored whey protein powder
   2 tablespoons hemp protein powder
   ½ bag baby spinach
   1 carrot, peeled
   ½–1 cup frozen fruit of your choice
   ½ tablespoon Omega-3 oil
   3 ice cubes
   ⅓ cup water

Throw all that shit in a blender and turn it on (but make sure you put the lid on first, dumbass). Rocket Fuel will make you feel like fucking Superman. The grosser it tastes, the better you'll feel and the bigger shits you'll take. Best enjoyed before or after weight training.

BULLSHIT METER: 1

SNACKS AND DESSERTS

FROZEN BANANAS

SERVES: *1*

Ingredients:
- 1 banana
- 1 freezer

Put a banana in the freezer—it tastes just like vanilla ice cream. I prefer to peel them first and store them in a sandwich bag, but you could throw one in there with the peel and wait for it to thaw before peeling. Whatever works.

BULLSHIT METER: 0

FROZEN GRAPES

SERVES: *It's a whole bag of grapes; that should make a lot of servings.*

Ingredients:
- 1 bag of grapes
- 1 freezer

Frozen grapes kick ass! Plus, freezing them is the only way to keep me from eating the whole damn bag at once. (If they're not frozen, I'll shove five grapes in my mouth at a time and the whole bag is gone in like two minutes.) When they're frozen, the process really slows down. This is excellent if you're a compulsive eater like me.

BULLSHIT METER: 0

APPLES AND PEANUT BUTTER
SERVES: *1*

Ingredients:
    1 apple (Fuji is my favorite)
    2 tablespoons all-natural peanut butter

If you can't figure this out, I can't help you. For everyone else, this is a great, healthy snack option. And if you live alone, you can eat the peanut butter right out of the jar! (Just don't eat the *whole* jar.)

BULLSHIT METER: 2 (Peanut butter has fat in it; it's healthy fat, but you still shouldn't overdo it.)

LÜC'S HOMEMADE PICKLES
SERVES: *I don't know . . . a lot.*

Ingredients:
    3 cucumbers, sliced
    1 bunch fresh dill, chopped
    ½ sweet onion, sliced (like onion rings)
    3 cloves garlic, minced
    2 teaspoons whole peppercorns
    1 teaspoon mustard seeds
    1½ cups water
    1 quart vinegar

Put the cucumbers, dill, onion, garlic, peppercorns, and mustard seeds in an 8-cup reusable plastic container. Add the water, then fill nearly to the brim with vinegar.

(continued)

You can eat these fuckers right away, but the longer you let them sit, the better they taste. It wouldn't kill you to throw in a little pickling salt or sea salt, but these are so damn good as a snack or on a sandwich that I like to eat them by the dozen, so I stay away from the sodium (and don't miss it in the least).

BULLSHIT METER: 3 (for the waiting factor)

DRINKS

THE LÜCARITA
SERVES: *1*

Ingredients:
   4-count of decent tequila ("1, 2, 3, 4, get your woman
      on the floor!")
   2-count soda water (not tonic water)
   2-count orange juice
   4 lemon wedges
   4 lime wedges

Pour the tequila, soda water, and orange juice in a shaker with ice. Squeeze the lemons and limes into the shaker, then toss in the rinds. Shake the hell out of it (I like to shake 18 times). Using a strainer, pour the drink over fresh ice. Enjoy!

BULLSHIT METER: 7 (A regular margarita has more than 500 calories and 20+ grams of sugar; mine has 150 calories and 8 grams of sugar.)

THE HALF DRINK

SERVES: 1

Ingredients:
  2-count decent vodka
  Soda water
  1 lime wedge

It's a vodka soda with half the booze. If I want to get drunk but I need to drop a couple pounds in preparation for a race, I'll switch to vodka sodas. The problem is, I pound them like water (because they taste like water). Next thing you know it's 40 minutes later and I'm being carried home on a stretcher. So I make them with half the booze, or pour them in a bigger glass with twice the soda water. This helps me get drunk at an average person's pace and avoid making a complete fool of myself.

BULLSHIT METER: 4

BLOODY MARY

SERVES: 1

Ingredients:
  4-count decent vodka
  4-count tomato juice
  Splash pickle juice
  4-splash regular Tabasco sauce
  Dash of salt
  Dash of black pepper
  1 pickled pepperoncini pepper

(continued)

Throw all the ingredients into a shaker with ice; shake well and serve in a highball glass. Garnish with a pickle spear or three green olives.

I don't know that I'd call this *healthy*, but it will save your life after a bender. There's a hell of a lot of salt in there, so don't drink more than two of these and drink plenty of water both before and after.

BULLSHIT METER: 8

Time Line

December 5, 1980: Birth

Spring 1990: Discovered Rock 'N' Roll.

Fall 1999: Went to college; started drinking. Heavily.

New Year's Eve, 1999: Smoked my first cigarette. Developed a nasty habit.

June 1, 2002: Dropped out of college; moved to NYC.

Spring 2003: Got hired at the taco shop.

Spring 2006: Started managing "the Clubhouse."

January 2009: Started dieting. One step closer to my new life.

February 2009: Gave up beer for nine long weeks. Lost 10 pounds in the first month.

Late February 2009: Went on my first "Rocky Run," 1.2 miles each way.

April 2009: Started writing down stories about trying to lose weight. *The Drunk Diet* is born.

May 2009: Gave up diet soda and cheese . . . on the same day. Down 25 pounds.

July 2009: Down 35 pounds.

August 2009: Ran over the Brooklyn Bridge for the first time. Kicked its ass. Down 40 pounds.

Thanksgiving 2009: Ran my first organized race. An 8K in New Jersey.

February 2010: Ran my first half-marathon.

March 2010: Quit smoking.

April 2010: Ran the Brooklyn half-marathon.

May 2010: Signed up for my first full marathon, still seven months away.

June–September 2010: Trained my ass off to run the marathon.

September 2010: Rode my bike from Boston to NYC (300 miles) to raise money for charity.

December 5, 2010: Ran my first full marathon, in Las Vegas. 3:56:55.

Lüc's Glossary

Cheeseburger (chēz-bər-gər): N. Female.
1. A sloppy, coked-up trash bag.
2. A girl to be enjoyed on rare occasions, usually alongside a bunch of beers on a Sunday afternoon.
Oh, that girl is a cheeseburger. I took her ass home last week; she wanted to stay up until eight A.M. doing coke, and she didn't have enough money left to take the subway home in the morning.

Dirty Ice Cream (Dər-tē Īs-Krēm): N. (Male or Female), V.
1. A person of the opposite sex whose first impression is much better than average, but then spoiled by calling and texting too much.
2. To call and text to the point of annoyance.
3. A partner that seems sweet in the beginning, but whom you quickly realized is tainted.
She's dirty ice cream. We went on one date and she's been blowing me up all fucking week.

Dump Truck (dump trək) N. Female.
1. A total slut with no class.
2. A truck with a bed that may be tilted to discharge its contents through an open tailgate.
"I can't believe you took home that dump truck last night. You better change your sheets."

French fry (french-frī) N. Male or Female.
1. A person who eats small portions of shitty food.
2. Someone who orders a Philly cheesesteak with steak fries and only picks at it, leaving almost the entire meal on the plate. This person is generally a drunkorexic consuming the majority of their daily calories in alcohol.

He's a French fry. We went to dinner last night and he didn't even touch the chicken, he only picked at the potatoes.

Meatball (mēt-böl): N. Female.
1. A deliciously thick girl with a big, fat, gorgeous ass. Generally has large tits and a small- to medium-sized midsection.
2. A *cheeseburger* that is not a *dump truck*.
"Oh, my God, did you see the size of the ass on the meatball over there at the bar?"

Vegetable (vej-tə-bəl): N. Female (could also be a nerdy Male).
1. A somewhat good-looking girl with a good head on her shoulders and no daddy issues, who has a real job and isn't an actress or model.
2. An attractive girl who reads a lot of books and has at least one cat.
She's pretty hot, but she's a vegetable; she just wants to watch Friends *all night and cuddle.*

Acknowledgments

M ost important, I'd like to start with my family. To Mom and Dad, for teaching me about hard work and that all good things in life—including love— are worth fighting for. To my brother, for being a huge asshole my entire life and for never being afraid to tell me how it is.

MY MOM DRESSED UP AS ME.

To Grandma Pryllis, Aunt Deb, and my cousin Matt Carl. Thank you all so much for believing in me, even when I had to talk you into it.

I'd like to thank all my boys in New York City that cheered me on to the finish line, even after they laughed at me when I told them I was writing a book (and laughed even harder when I told them the title): Brian Newman; Georgie Seville, who taught me everything I know about the nightclub industry (and thanks for letting me use your bar for the cover photo shoot); Marty E., who taught me how to drink; Tommy London, who taught me that Rock 'N' Roll is a dream and sometimes you have to wake up and make it happen; Ian Eldorado; Freddy the Necktie, for doing security for free beers; Lady Starlight; TJ the J; Kurt Stevens, for teaching me more about Rock 'N' Roll than I could ever possibly remember. My best friends for life. I'd take a bullet for you fuckers, then I'd shoot you for putting me in another shitty situation. And to Jenna, who is responsible for my hair and is therefore indirectly responsible for everything I've accomplished in my life.

Thank you to all my friends back in Nebraska, who have put up with all my bullshit ever since I was a kid: Chris Bivens; Pat Minturn; Royce, for coming to all of my big races and for taking care of Ginger for me; Brian Eaton; Vinny G; and most of all, Ryan Bivens, who has been my best friend since I had my very first beer.

Thank you to the owners of all the shit-holes I've worked in over the last ten years for underpaying me, overworking me, and making me fight harder every single day just to earn a decent living. To Lisa, Brent, Drew, Seth, Ashley, the Dirt, Troy, and the enormous cast of characters I've met along the way. (That doesn't mean I want you to call me.)

To my bike, Delilah, who started it all; my new bike, Karen, who spends long hours with me; and to the fine people at Soul Cycle for keeping me sane on my days off from running. To my running shoes, who are right there with me literally every step of the way. I cry when I throw a pair of you away every two months. And to Linda, the psychologist behind the counter at my gym, who was there for every pound, every step, every weight I lifted, and every French fry I turned down. And to the New York Road Runners, of which I am a very proud member.

To Brittney, who found a guy with a Web site and crazy hair and decided to believe in him. Without her, *The Drunk Diet* would still be sitting on my desk, stapled together. To my editor, Kathy Huck, I told you this was for real, and you believed me; Steve Cohen, for taking me golfing; John Murphy; Sally Richardson; and the entire St. Martin's crew, for taking a chance on a Rock 'N' Roller born two decades too late. To Courtney Hargrave, who made my crazy ideas more reader-friendly. To Kelly McNees; Maya Contreras, who talked me into writing my first sentence while we were having piña coladas; and Elizabeth Houston. To Claudia Ballard, my agent at WME, who told me my book was good even though I didn't believe her. And Troy Carter.

To Josh, who I text incessantly about running and who never asks for anything in return—the only person I've ever met who can drink and run as much as I can. Hopefully one day I won't be staring at the back of your head the whole damn race, you asshole.

To Budweiser and Jameson. Without the two of you, I would never have gotten all of these incredibly ridiculous ideas.

To anyone who has ever been to my Web site, even if you

never came back. And to everyone who follows my insanity on Twitter.

To all the people who pissed me off along the way: Without you, I'd still be selling tacos.

To anyone who has ever had the balls to put on a pair of running shoes and put one foot in front of the other.

And to anyone I've forgotten, go fuck yourself.

Index